INVESTIGATIONS IN NUMBER, DATA, AND SPACE®

Estimating and Measuring

Measurement Benchmarks

Grade 5

Also appropriate for Grade 6

Cornelia Tierney
Margie Singer
Marlene Kliman
Megan Murray

Developed at TERC, Cambridge, Massachusetts

Dale Seymour Publications®
White Plains, New York

The *Investigations* curriculum was developed at TERC (formerly Technical Education Research Centers) in collaboration with Kent State University and the State University of New York at Buffalo. The work was supported in part by National Science Foundation Grant No. ESI-9050210. TERC is a nonprofit company working to improve mathematics and science education. TERC is located at 2067 Massachusetts Avenue, Cambridge, MA 02140.

This project was supported, in part,
by the

National Science Foundation

Opinions expressed are those of the authors
and not necessarily those of the Foundation

Managing Editor: Catherine Anderson

Series Editor: Beverly Cory

Revision Team: Laura Marshall Alavosus, Ellen Harding, Patty Green Holubar, Suzanne Knott, Beverly Hersh Lozoff

ESL Consultant: Nancy Sokol Green

Production/Manufacturing Director: Janet Yearian

Production/Manufacturing Supervisor: Karen Edmonds

Production/Manufacturing Coordinator: Barbara Atmore

Design Manager: Jeff Kelly

Design: Don Taka

Illustrations: DJ Simison, Carl Yoshihara

Cover: Bay Graphics

Composition: Archetype Book Composition

This book is published by Dale Seymour Publications®, an imprint of Addison Wesley Longman, Inc.

Dale Seymour Publications
10 Bank Street
White Plains, NY 10602
Customer Service: 1-800-872-1100

Order number DS47048
ISBN 1-57232-801-0
2 3 4 5 6 7 8 9 10-ML-02 01 00 99 98

Printed on Recycled Paper

T E R C

Principal Investigator   Susan Jo Russell

Co-Principal Investigator   Cornelia Tierney

Director of Research and Evaluation   Jan Mokros

Curriculum Development
Joan Akers
Michael T. Battista
Mary Berle-Carman
Douglas H. Clements
Karen Economopoulos
Claryce Evans
Marlene Kliman
Cliff Konold
Jan Mokros
Megan Murray
Ricardo Nemirovsky
Tracy Noble
Andee Rubin
Susan Jo Russell
Margie Singer
Cornelia Tierney

Evaluation and Assessment
Mary Berle-Carman
Jan Mokros
Andee Rubin
Tracey Wright

Teacher Support
Kabba Colley
Karen Economopoulos
Anne Goodrow
Nancy Ishihara
Liana Laughlin
Jerrie Moffett
Megan Murray
Margie Singer
Dewi Win
Virginia Woolley
Tracey Wright
Lisa Yaffee

Administration and Production
Irene Baker
Amy Catlin
Amy Taber

**Cooperating Classrooms
for This Unit**
Barbara Fox
Leslie Kramer
Sarah Novogrodsky
*Cambridge Public Schools
Cambridge, MA*

Technology Development
Michael T. Battista
Douglas H. Clements
Ricardo Nemirovsky
Tracy Noble
Julie Sarama

Video Production
David A. Smith

Consultants and Advisors
Deborah Lowenberg Ball
Marilyn Burns
Mary Johnson
James J. Kaput
Mary M. Lindquist
Leslie P. Steffe
Grayson Wheatley

Graduate Assistants
Richard Aistrope
Kathryn Battista
Caroline Borrow
William Hunt
Kent State University

Jeffrey Barrett
Julie Sarama
Sudha Swaminathan
Elaine Vukelic
State University of New York at Buffalo

Dan Gillette
Irene Hall
Harvard Graduate School of Education

Revisions and Home Materials
Cathy Miles Grant
Marlene Kliman
Margaret McGaffigan
Megan Murray
Kim O'Neil
Andee Rubin
Susan Jo Russell
Lisa Seyferth
Myriam Steinback
Judy Storeygard
Anna Suarez
Cornelia Tierney
Carol Walker
Tracey Wright

CONTENTS

WHERE TO START

The first-time user of *Measurement Benchmarks* should read the following:

When you next teach this same unit, you can begin to read more of the background. Each time you present the unit, you will learn more about how your students understand the mathematical ideas.

Investigations in Number, Data, and Space® is a K–5 mathematics curriculum with four major goals:

■ to offer students meaningful mathematical problems

■ to emphasize depth in mathematical thinking rather than superficial exposure to a series of fragmented topics

■ to communicate mathematics content and pedagogy to teachers

■ to substantially expand the pool of mathematically literate students

The *Investigations* curriculum embodies a new approach based on years of research about how children learn mathematics. Each grade level consists of a set of separate units, each offering 2–8 weeks of work. These units of study are presented through investigations that involve students in the exploration of major mathematical ideas.

Approaching the mathematics content through investigations helps students develop flexibility and confidence in approaching problems, fluency in using mathematical skills and tools to solve problems, and proficiency in evaluating their solutions. Students also build a repertoire of ways to communicate about their mathematical thinking, while their enjoyment and appreciation of mathematics grows.

The investigations are carefully designed to invite all students into mathematics—girls and boys, members of diverse cultural, ethnic, and language groups, and students with different strengths and interests. Problem contexts often call on students to share experiences from their family, culture, or community. The curriculum eliminates barriers—such as work in isolation from peers, or emphasis on speed and memorization—that exclude some students from participating successfully in mathematics. The following aspects of the curriculum ensure that all students are included in significant mathematics learning:

■ Students spend time exploring problems in depth.

■ They find more than one solution to many of the problems they work on.

■ They invent their own strategies and approaches, rather than rely on memorized procedures.

■ They choose from a variety of concrete materials and appropriate technology, including calculators, as a natural part of their everyday mathematical work.

■ They express their mathematical thinking through drawing, writing, and talking.

■ They work in a variety of groupings—as a whole class, individually, in pairs, and in small groups.

■ They move around the classroom as they explore the mathematics in their environment and talk with their peers.

While reading and other language activities are typically given a great deal of time and emphasis in elementary classrooms, mathematics often does not get the time it needs. If students are to experience mathematics in depth, they must have enough time to become engaged in real mathematical problems. We believe that a minimum of 5 hours of mathematics classroom time a week—about an hour a day—is critical at the elementary level. The scope and pacing of the *Investigations* curriculum are based on that belief.

We explain more about the pedagogy and principles that underlie these investigations in Teacher Notes throughout the units. For correlations of the curriculum to the NCTM Standards and further help in using this research-based program for teaching mathematics, see the following books, available from Dale Seymour Publications:

■ *Implementing the* Investigations in Number, Data, and Space® *Curriculum*

■ *Beyond Arithmetic: Changing Mathematics in the Elementary Classroom* by Jan Mokros, Susan Jo Russell, and Karen Economopoulos

This book is one of the curriculum units for *Investigations in Number, Data, and Space.* In addition to providing part of a complete mathematics curriculum for your students, this unit offers information to support your own professional development. You, the teacher, are the person who will make this curriculum come alive in the classroom; the book for each unit is your main support system.

Although the curriculum does not include student textbooks, reproducible sheets for student work are provided in the unit and are also available as Student Activity Booklets. Students work actively with objects and experiences in their own environment and with a variety of manipulative materials and technology, rather than with a book of instruction and problems. We strongly recommend use of the overhead projector as a way to present problems, to focus group discussion, and to help students share ideas and strategies.

Ultimately, every teacher will use these investigations in ways that make sense for his or her particular style, the particular group of students, and the constraints and supports of a particular school environment. Each unit offers information and guidance for a wide variety of situations, drawn from our collaborations with many teachers and students over many years. Our goal in this book is to help you, a professional educator, implement this curriculum in a way that will give all your students access to mathematical power.

Investigation Format

The opening two pages of each investigation help you get ready for the work that follows.

What Happens This gives a synopsis of each session or block of sessions.

Mathematical Emphasis This lists the most important ideas and processes students will encounter in this investigation.

What to Plan Ahead of Time These lists alert you to materials to gather, sheets to duplicate, transparencies to make, and anything else you need to do before starting.

It's About Time

What Happens

Session 1: Estimating Half a Minute Students make a list of units for measuring time and begin to chart benchmarks they already use for any of these units. Then they estimate the passage of 30 seconds and graph how their estimates change with increased practice.

Session 2: Commercial Minutes Students analyze data collected at home on the number of commercial minutes in a half-hour television show. They use their data and national statistics to estimate how much time an average fifth grader spends watching commercials each year.

Session 3: Making Sense of Years Students compare people's ages in two ways: "how many years older" and "how many times as old." They make strips out of one-centimeter graph paper to represent the years of their lives to date, and the lives of adults whose ages they have learned. They use these strips in making age comparisons.

Mathematical Emphasis

■ Developing vocabulary for units of time
■ Developing benchmarks for minutes and for years
■ Timing in minutes and seconds
■ Collecting, displaying, and analyzing data
■ Using measurement conversions (minutes to hours to days) in the problem-solving process
■ Keeping track of computations in a multistep problem

What to Plan Ahead of Time

Materials

■ Clock or watch with a second hand: 1 per small group, or use the classroom clock (Session 1)
■ Calculators: 1 per pair (Sessions 2–3)
■ Overhead projector (Session 2, optional)
■ Scissors (Session 3)
■ Tape (Session 3)
■ Chart paper (Sessions 1, 3)

Other Preparation

■ Duplicate student sheets and teaching resources (located at the end of this unit) in the following quantities. If you have Student Activity Booklets, no copying is needed.

For Session 1
Student Sheet 20, Estimating 30 Seconds (p. 120): 1 per student
Student Sheet 21, Commercial Minutes (p. 121): 1 per student (homework)

For Session 2
Student Sheet 22, Adults' Ages (p. 122): 1 per student (homework)

For Session 3
Student Sheet 23, Comparing Ages (p. 123): 1 per student
One-centimeter graph paper (p. 124): 2–3 sheets per student

■ Review the process of making a line plot. Refer to the **Teacher Note**, Sketch Graphs: Quick to Make, Easy to Read, p. 73. (Session 2)

■ Cut strips of centimeter paper (1 cm = 1 year), making demonstration "lifetime" strips to represent the ages of an adult and a child in your life. Pick a child younger than your students. (Session 3)

Sessions Within an investigation, the activities are organized by class session, a session being at least a one-hour math class. Sessions are numbered consecutively through an investigation. Often several sessions are grouped together, presenting a block of activities with a single major focus.

When you find a block of sessions presented together—for example, Sessions 1, 2, and 3—read through the entire block first to understand the overall flow and sequence of the activities. Make some preliminary decisions about how you will divide the activities into three sessions for your class, based on what you know about your students. You may need to modify your initial plans as you progress through the activities, and you may want to make notes in the margins of the pages as reminders for the next time you use the unit.

Be sure to read the Session Follow-Up section at the end of the session block to see what homework assignments and extensions are suggested as you make your initial plans.

While you may be used to a curriculum that tells you exactly what each class session should cover, we have found that the teacher is in a better position to make these decisions. Each unit is flexible and may be handled somewhat differently by every teacher. Although we provide guidance for how many sessions a particular group of activities is likely to need, we want you to be active in determining an appropriate pace and the best transition points for your class. It is not unusual for a teacher to spend more or less time than is proposed for the activities.

Ten-Minute Math At the beginning of some sessions, you will find Ten-Minute Math activities. These are designed to be used in tandem with the investigations, but not during the math hour. Rather, we hope you will do them whenever you have a spare 10 minutes—maybe before lunch or recess, or at the end of the day.

Ten-Minute Math offers practice in key concepts, but not always those being covered in the unit. For example, in a unit on using data, Ten-Minute Math might revisit geometric activities done earlier in the year. Complete directions for the suggested activities are included at the end of each unit.

Session 1

Estimating Half a Minute

Materials

- Chart paper
- Clock or watch with a second hand (1 per group)
- Student Sheet 20 (1 per student)
- Student Sheet 21 (1 per student, homework)

What Happens

Students make a list of units for measuring time and begin to chart benchmarks they already use for any of these units. Then they estimate the passage of 30 seconds and graph how their estimates change with increased practice. Their work focuses on:

- developing benchmarks for units of time
- using an analog clock to time in seconds
- estimating 30 seconds
- graphing repeated trials

Ten-Minute Math: Guess My Unit Once or twice during this investigation, outside of math class, continue to play Guess My Unit, the variation of Guess My Number that was introduced as Ten-Minute Math for Investigation 2 (see p. 58). As needed, restore the cards for units of time for use during this investigation.

Activity

Discussion: Units of Time

Measures of Time	
Units	Benchmarks

In preparation for this brief introductory discussion, make a two-column chart titled *Measures of Time*. Label one column *Units* and the other *Benchmarks*. Post the paper in a convenient place, possibly with your other "Measures" charts, so that students may refer and add to it throughout this investigation.

So far in this unit we've measured length and distance—how long or how far away something is. We've measured weight—how heavy things are—and we've measured liquid quantities. Now we're going to talk about *time*. Is time something we can measure? How? What are some units we use to measure time?

Record students' suggestions on the chart. Common time measures such as *second, minute, hour, day, week, month,* and *year* will probably be on your list. There are less common measures that might intrigue some students, including *fortnight, decade, century,* and *millennium*. Introduce some of these by using them in a familiar context (for example, "We live in the twentieth century.") and discuss what they mean.

76 ■ Investigation 3: It's About Time

Activities The activities include pair and small-group work, individual tasks, and whole-class discussions. In any case, students are seated together, talking and sharing ideas during all work times. Students most often work cooperatively, although each student may record work individually.

Choice Time In some units, some sessions are structured with activity choices. In these cases, students may work simultaneously on different activities focused on the same mathematical ideas. Students choose which activities they want to do, and they cycle through them.

You will need to decide how to set up and introduce these activities and how to let students make their choices. Some teachers present them as station activities, in different parts of the room. Some list the choices on the board as reminders or have students keep their own lists.

Tips for the Linguistically Diverse Classroom At strategic points in each unit, you will find concrete suggestions for simple modifications of the teaching strategies to encourage the participation of all students. Many of these tips offer alternative ways to elicit critical thinking from students at varying levels of English proficiency, as well as from other students who find it difficult to verbalize their thinking.

The tips are supported by suggestions for specific vocabulary work to help ensure that all students can participate fully in the investigations. The Preview for the Linguistically Diverse Classroom lists important words that are assumed as part of the working vocabulary of the unit. Second-language learners will need to become familiar with these words in order to understand the problems and activities they will be doing. These terms can be incorporated into students' second-language work before or during the unit. Activities that can be used to present the words are found in the appendix, Vocabulary Support for Second-Language Learners. In addition, ideas for making connections to students' languages and cultures, included on the Preview page, help the class explore the unit's concepts from a multicultural perspective.

Session Follow-Up: Homework   In *Investigations,* homework is an extension of classroom work. Sometimes it offers review and practice of work done in class, sometimes preparation for upcoming activities, and sometimes numerical practice that revisits work in earlier units. Homework plays a role both in supporting students' learning and in helping inform families about the ways in which students in this curriculum work with mathematical ideas.

Depending on your school's homework policies and your own judgment, you may want to assign more homework than is suggested in the units. For this purpose you might use the practice pages, included as blackline masters at the end of this unit, to give students additional work with numbers.

For some homework assignments, you will want to adapt the activity to meet the needs of a variety of students in your class: those with special needs, those ready for more challenge, and second-language learners. You might change the numbers in a problem, make the activity more or less complex, or go through a sample activity with

those who need extra help. You can modify any student sheet for either homework or class use. In particular, making numbers in a problem smaller or larger can make the same basic activity appropriate for a wider range of students.

Another issue to consider is how to handle the homework that students bring back to class—how to recognize the work they have done at home without spending too much time on it. Some teachers hold a short group discussion of different approaches to the assignment; others ask students to share and discuss their work with a neighbor; still others post the homework around the room and give students time to tour it briefly. If you want to keep track of homework students bring in, be sure it ends up in a designated place.

Session Follow-Up: Extensions   Sometimes in Session Follow-Up, you will find suggested extension activities. These are opportunities for some or all students to explore a topic in greater depth or in a different context. They are not designed for "fast" students; mathematics is a multifaceted discipline, and different students will want to go further in different investigations. Look for and encourage the sparks of interest and enthusiasm you see in your students, and use the extensions to help them pursue these interests.

Excursions   Some of the *Investigations* units include excursions—blocks of activities that could be omitted without harming the integrity of the unit. This is one way of dealing with the great depth and variety of elementary mathematics— much more than a class has time to explore in any one year. Excursions give you the flexibility to make different choices from year to year, doing the excursion in one unit this time, and next year trying another excursion.

Materials

A complete list of the materials needed for teaching this unit follows the unit overview. Some of these materials are available in kits for the *Investigations* curriculum. Individual items can also be purchased from school supply dealers.

Classroom Materials   In an active mathematics classroom, certain basic materials should be available at all times: interlocking cubes, pencils, unlined paper, graph paper, calculators, things to count with, and measuring tools. Some activities in this curriculum require scissors and glue sticks or tape. Stick-on notes and large paper are also useful materials throughout.

So that students can independently get what they need at any time, they should know where these materials are kept, how they are stored, and how they are to be returned to the storage area. For example, interlocking cubes are best stored in towers of ten; then, whatever the activity, they should be returned to storage in groups of ten at the end of the hour. You'll find that establishing such routines at the beginning of the year is well worth the time and effort.

Student Sheets and Teaching Resources   Student recording sheets and other teaching tools needed for both class and homework are provided as reproducible blackline masters at the end of each unit. We think it's important that students find their own ways of organizing and recording their work. They need to learn how to explain their thinking with both drawings and written words, and how to organize their results so someone else can understand them. For this reason, we deliberately do not provide student sheets for every activity. Regardless of the form in which students do their work, we recommend that they keep their

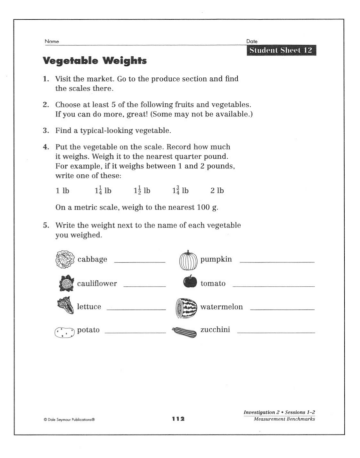

work in a mathematics folder, journal, or notebook so that it is always available to them for reference.

Student Activity Booklets   These booklets contain all the sheets each student will need for individual work, freeing you from extensive copying (although you may need or want to copy the occasional teaching resource on transparency film or card stock, or make extra copies of a student sheet).

Calculators and Computers   Calculators are used throughout *Investigations*. Many of the units recommend that you have at least one calculator for each pair. You will find calculator activities, plus Teacher Notes discussing this important mathematical tool, in an early unit at each grade level. It is assumed that calculators will be readily available for student use.

Computer activities are offered at all grade levels. How you use the computer activities depends on the number of computers you have available. Technology in the Curriculum discusses ways to incorporate the use of calculators and computers into classroom activities.

Children's Literature Each unit offers a list of related children's literature that can be used to support the mathematical ideas in the unit. Sometimes an activity is based on a specific children's book, with suggestions for substitutions where practical. While such activities can be adapted and taught without the book, the literature offers a rich introduction and should be used whenever possible.

***Investigations* at Home** It is a good idea to make your policy on homework explicit to both students and their families when you begin teaching with *Investigations*. How frequently will you be assigning homework? When do you expect homework to be completed and brought back to school? What are your goals in assigning homework? How independent should families expect their children to be? What should the parent's or guardian's role be? The more explicit you can be about your expectations, the better the homework experience will be for everyone.

Investigations at Home (a booklet available separately for each unit, to send home with students) gives you a way to communicate with families about the work students are doing in class. This booklet includes a brief description of every session, a list of the mathematics content emphasized in each investigation, and a discussion of each homework assignment to help families more effectively support their children. Whether or not you are using the *Investigations* at Home booklets, we expect you to make your own choices about homework assignments. Feel free to omit any and to add extra ones you think are appropriate.

Family Letter A letter that you can send home to students' families is included with the blackline masters for each unit. Families need to be informed about the mathematics work in your classroom; they should be encouraged to participate in and support their children's work. A reminder to send home the letter for each unit appears in one of the early investigations. These letters are also available separately in Spanish, Vietnamese, Cantonese, Hmong, and Cambodian.

Help for You, the Teacher

Because we believe strongly that a new curriculum must help teachers think in new ways about mathematics and about their students' mathematical thinking processes, we have included a great deal of material to help you learn more about both.

About the Mathematics in This Unit This introductory section summarizes the critical information about the mathematics you will be teaching. It describes the unit's central mathematical ideas and the ways students will encounter them through the unit's activities.

About the Assessment in this Unit This introductory section highlights Teacher Checkpoints and assessment activities contained in the unit. It offers questions to stimulate your assessment as you observe the development of students' mathematical thinking and learning.

Teacher Notes These reference notes provide practical information about the mathematics you are teaching and about our experience with how students learn. Many of the notes were written in response to actual questions from teachers or to discuss important things we saw happening in the

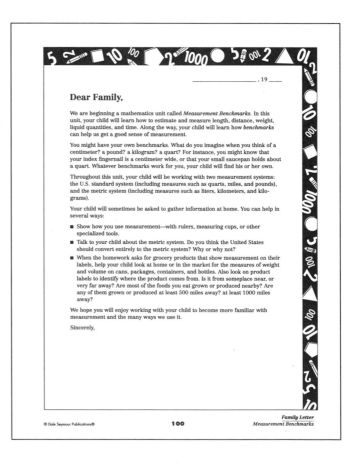

_____ , 19 ___

Dear Family,

We are beginning a mathematics unit called *Measurement Benchmarks*. In this unit, your child will learn how to estimate and measure length, distance, weight, liquid quantities, and time. Along the way, your child will learn how *benchmarks* can help us get a good sense of measurement.

You might have your own benchmarks. What do you imagine when you think of a centimeter? a pound? a kilogram? a quart? For instance, you might know that your index fingernail is a centimeter wide, or that your small saucepan holds about a quart. Whatever benchmarks work for you, your child will find his or her own.

Throughout this unit, your child will be working with two measurement systems: the U.S. standard system (including measures such as quarts, miles, and pounds), and the metric system (including measures such as liters, kilometers, and kilograms).

Your child will sometimes be asked to gather information at home. You can help in several ways:

■ Show how you use measurement—with rulers, measuring cups, or other specialized tools.

■ Talk to your child about the metric system. Do you think the United States should convert entirely to the metric system? Why or why not?

■ When the homework asks for grocery products that show measurement on their labels, help your child look at home or in the market for the measures of weight and volume on cans, packages, containers, and bottles. Also look on product labels to identify where the product comes from. Is it from someplace near, or very far away? Are most of the foods you eat grown or produced nearby? Are any of them grown or produced at least 500 miles away? at least 1000 miles away?

We hope you will enjoy working with your child to become more familiar with measurement and the many ways we use it.

Sincerely,

© Dale Seymour Publications®   **100**   *Family Letter*
Measurement Benchmarks

field-test classrooms. Some teachers like to read them all before starting the unit, then review them as they come up in particular investigations.

Dialogue Boxes Sample dialogues demonstrate how students typically express their mathematical ideas, what issues and confusions arise in their thinking, and how some teachers have guided class discussions.

These dialogues are based on the extensive classroom testing of this curriculum; many are word-for-word transcriptions of recorded class discussions. They are not always easy reading; sometimes it may take some effort to unravel what the students are trying to say. But this is the value

of these dialogues; they offer good clues to how your students may develop and express their approaches and strategies, helping you prepare for your own class discussions.

Where to Start You may not have time to read everything the first time you use this unit. As a first-time user, you will likely focus on understanding the activities and working them out with your students. Read completely through all the activities before starting to present them. Also read those sections listed in the Contents under the heading Where to Start.

Teacher Note ⟩ *Introducing Benchmarks*

A benchmark is something familiar that is about the same size as a particular unit of measurement. We can use benchmarks to help estimate the size of something when a measuring tool is not handy. For example, if we know that the nail of our index finger is about a centimeter wide, we can use it to estimate length in centimeters. We can also use benchmarks to help us understand and remember the size of a measurement unit.

When introducing benchmarks to the class, encourage students to share ways that measurement units have become meaningful to them. In one class, the teacher began by telling a story about a benchmark of her own:

"When I was a little girl, I lived in a house that was on top of a hill. My mother was a wonderful cook. She loved to bake. A lot of times, she'd be in the middle of baking and she would run out of an ingredient. She used to send me to the store for 5-pound bags of sugar or flour. If I think back to walking up that hill with that bag, I have a memory of what 5 pounds feels like. So now whenever somebody tells me that something weighs around 5 pounds, I remember what it felt like to carry those 5-pound bags of sugar up that hill."

After the teacher told her story, she invited other students to share their own stories about familiar benchmarks. Several students shared ways that they found meaning for a mile:

Manuel: When you walk a mile, it takes about half an hour. When my mom and I run together on Saturdays, we go four times around the track to make a mile. I don't know how long it takes, but I get really tired!

Lindsay: I like watching the odometer in the car when my parents drive. Sometimes I time how long it takes to go a mile. It takes about a minute when we're on the highway, but sometimes when we're in traffic it takes a minute and a half or two minutes or even longer.

Shakita: It's a mile to downtown from school. I know because I bike downtown to my flute lesson after school every Thursday.

Noah: I used to live in New York City, and there a wide city block is about a tenth of a mile, so when you walk ten blocks across town, you go a mile. And when you walk on the short blocks going up and down it takes twenty blocks to go a mile.

The more that students can bring their out-of-school experiences into math class, the more meaningful and engaging learning will be. As students share the ways that they have come to develop their own benchmarks, they develop new insights about the meaning of measurement units.

D I A L O G U E □ B O X

Ordering Our Products by Metric Weights

As these students are lining up in order by the weight of the contents of their packages (p. 50), they reason about where along the wall they should stand. Their teacher has posted signs along the wall to mark positions for 0 grams, 500 grams, and 1000 grams. Students found themselves clustered near the 500-gram sign.

Katrina: I know I'm going to go close to the 500 sign that Ms. Lopez put up, because I have one that's 454 grams, and that's pretty close to 500.

Leon: So do I! Mine's 454 too.

Becky: And I have one that says 453, so I'll go right before the two of you.

Duc: Mine only says 1 pound. How am I supposed to find my spot?

Mei-Ling: Mine says a pound *and* 454 grams, so they must be the same.

Duc: So I go here too. There's a lot of us.

Kevin: Well, it makes sense that there's a lot of us around there. We found a lot of cans that were about a pound, and a pound is 454 grams.

Becky: Wait. Mine says a pound too, and it says 453 grams. How can that be?

Amy Lynn: It's close. Maybe it's not exactly a pound, and they just rounded it up.

Desiree: Mine only has ounces on it. How do I figure out how many grams are in 10 ounces?

Duc: One ounce is about 28 grams, that should help.

Desiree: If one ounce is 28 grams, then 10 ounces would have to be 280 grams because it's like timesing by 10, you just add a zero.

Greg: Your cereal box can't be only 280 grams. It's enormous! My bag is 300 grams, and it's much smaller.

Desiree: I know this box looks big, but it's 10 ounces, and that means it's not even 300 grams.

The *Investigations* curriculum incorporates the use of two forms of technology in the classroom: calculators and computers. Calculators are assumed to be standard classroom materials, available for student use in any unit. Computers are explicitly linked to one or more units at each grade level; they are used with the unit on 2-D geometry at each grade, as well as with some of the units on measuring, data, and changes.

Using Calculators

In this curriculum, calculators are considered tools for doing mathematics, similar to pattern blocks or interlocking cubes. Just as with other tools, students must learn both *how* to use calculators correctly and *when* they are appropriate to use. This knowledge is crucial for daily life, as calculators are now a standard way of handling numerical operations, both at work and at home.

Using a calculator correctly is not a simple task; it depends on a good knowledge of the four operations and of the number system, so that students can select suitable calculations and also determine what a reasonable result would be. These skills are the basis of any work with numbers, whether or not a calculator is involved.

Unfortunately, calculators are often seen as tools to check computations with, as if other methods are somehow more fallible. Students need to understand that any computational method can be used to check any other; it's just as easy to make a mistake on the calculator as it is to make a mistake on paper or with mental arithmetic. Throughout this curriculum, we encourage students to solve computation problems in more than one way in order to double-check their accuracy. We present mental arithmetic, paper-and-pencil computation, and calculators as three possible approaches.

In this curriculum we also recognize that, despite their importance, calculators are not always appropriate in mathematics instruction. Like any tools, calculators are useful for some tasks but not for others. You will need to make decisions about when to allow students access to calculators and when to ask that they solve problems without them so that they can concentrate on other tools and skills. At times when calculators are or are not appropriate for a particular activity, we make specific recommendations. Help your students develop their own sense of which problems they can tackle with their own reasoning and which ones might be better solved with a combination of their own reasoning and the calculator.

Managing calculators in your classroom so that they are a tool, and not a distraction, requires some planning. When calculators are first introduced, students often want to use them for everything, even problems that can be solved quite simply by other methods. However, once the novelty wears off, students are just as interested in developing their own strategies, especially when these strategies are emphasized and valued in the classroom. Over time, students will come to recognize the ease and value of solving problems mentally, with paper and pencil, or with manipulatives, while also understanding the power of the calculator to facilitate work with larger numbers.

Experience shows that if calculators are available only occasionally, students become excited and distracted when they are permitted to use them. They focus on the tool rather than on the mathematics. In order to learn when calculators are appropriate and when they are not, students must have easy access to them and use them routinely in their work.

If you have a calculator for each student, and if you think your students can accept the responsibility, you might allow them to keep their calculators with the rest of their individual materials, at least for the first few weeks of school. Alternatively, you might store them in boxes on a shelf, number each calculator, and assign a corresponding number to each student. This system can give students a sense of ownership while also helping you keep track of the calculators.

Using Computers

Students can use computers to approach and visualize mathematical situations in new ways. The computer allows students to construct and manipulate geometric shapes, see objects move according to rules they specify, and turn, flip, and repeat a pattern.

This curriculum calls for computers in units where they are a particularly effective tool for learning mathematics content. One unit on 2-D geometry at each of the grades 3–5 includes a core of activities that rely on access to computers, either in the classroom or in a lab. Other units on geometry, measuring, data, and changes include computer activities, but can be taught without them. In these units, however, students' experience is greatly enhanced by computer use.

The following list outlines the recommended use of computers in this curriculum:

Kindergarten
Unit: *Making Shapes and Building Blocks*
  (Exploring Geometry)
Software: *Shapes*
Source: provided with the unit

Grade 1
Unit: *Survey Questions and Secret Rules*
  (Collecting and Sorting Data)
Software: *Tabletop, Jr.*
Source: Broderbund

Unit: *Quilt Squares and Block Towns*
  (2-D and 3-D Geometry)
Software: *Shapes*
Source: provided with the unit

Grade 2
Unit: *Mathematical Thinking at Grade 2*
  (Introduction)
Software: *Shapes*
Source: provided with the unit

Unit: *Shapes, Halves, and Symmetry*
  (Geometry and Fractions)
Software: *Shapes*
Source: provided with the unit

Unit: *How Long? How Far?* (Measuring)
Software: *Geo-Logo*
Source: provided with the unit

Grade 3
Unit: *Flips, Turns, and Area* (2-D Geometry)
Software: *Tumbling Tetrominoes*
Source: provided with the unit

Unit: *Turtle Paths* (2-D Geometry)
Software: *Geo-Logo*
Source: provided with the unit

Grade 4
Unit: *Sunken Ships and Grid Patterns*
  (2-D Geometry)
Software: *Geo-Logo*
Source: provided with the unit

Grade 5
Unit: *Picturing Polygons* (2-D Geometry)
Software: *Geo-Logo*
Source: provided with the unit

Unit: *Patterns of Change* (Tables and Graphs)
Software: *Trips*
Source: provided with the unit

Unit: *Data: Kids, Cats, and Ads* (Statistics)
Software: *Tabletop, Sr.*
Source: Broderbund

The software provided with the *Investigations* units uses the power of the computer to help students explore mathematical ideas and relationships that cannot be explored in the same way with physical materials. With the *Shapes* (grades 1–2) and *Tumbling Tetrominoes* (grade 3) software, students explore symmetry, pattern, rotation and reflection, area, and characteristics of 2-D shapes. With the *Geo-Logo* software (grades 2–5), students investigate rotations and reflections, coordinate geometry, the properties of 2-D shapes, and angles. The *Trips* software (grade 5) is a mathematical exploration of motion in which students run experiments and interpret data presented in graphs and tables.

We suggest that students work in pairs on the computer; this not only maximizes computer resources but also encourages students to consult, monitor, and teach each other. Generally, more than two students at one computer find it difficult to share. Managing access to computers is an issue for every classroom. The curriculum gives you explicit support for setting up a system. The units are structured on the assumption that you have enough computers for half your students to work on the machines in pairs at one time. If you do not have access to that many computers, suggestions are made for structuring class time to use the unit with fewer than five.

Assessment plays a critical role in teaching and learning, and it is an integral part of the *Investigations* curriculum. For a teacher using these units, assessment is an ongoing process. You observe students' discussions and explanations of their strategies on a daily basis and examine their work as it evolves. While students are busy recording and representing their work, working on projects, sharing with partners, and playing mathematical games, you have many opportunities to observe their mathematical thinking. What you learn through observation guides your decisions about how to proceed. In any of the units, you will repeatedly consider questions like these:

- Do students come up with their own strategies for solving problems, or do they expect others to tell them what to do? What do their strategies reveal about their mathematical understanding?

- Do students understand that there are different strategies for solving problems? Do they articulate their strategies and try to understand other students' strategies?

- How effectively do students use materials as tools to help with their mathematical work?

- Do students have effective ideas for keeping track of and recording their work? Do keeping track of and recording their work seem difficult for them?

You will need to develop a comfortable and efficient system for recording and keeping track of your observations. Some teachers keep a clipboard handy and jot notes on a class list or on adhesive labels that are later transferred to student files. Others keep loose-leaf notebooks with a page for each student and make weekly notes about what they have observed in class.

Assessment Tools in the Unit

With the activities in each unit, you will find questions to guide your thinking while observing the students at work. You will also find two built-in assessment tools: Teacher Checkpoints and embedded Assessment activities.

Teacher Checkpoints   The designated Teacher Checkpoints in each unit offer a time to "check in" with individual students, watch them at work, and ask questions that illuminate how they are thinking.

At first it may be hard to know what to look for, hard to know what kinds of questions to ask. Students may be reluctant to talk; they may not be accustomed to having the teacher ask them about their work, or they may not know how to explain their thinking. Two important ingredients of this process are asking students open-ended questions about their work and showing genuine interest in how they are approaching the task. When students see that you are interested in their thinking and are counting on them to come up with their own ways of solving problems, they may surprise you with the depth of their understanding.

Teacher Checkpoints also give you the chance to pause in the teaching sequence and reflect on how your class is doing overall. Think about whether you need to adjust your pacing: Are most students fluent with strategies for solving a particular kind of problem? Are they just starting to formulate good strategies? Or are they still struggling with how to start? Depending on what you see as the students work, you may want to spend more time on similar problems, change some of the problems to use smaller numbers, move quickly to more-challenging material, modify subsequent activities for some students, work on particular ideas with a small group, or pair students who have good strategies with those who are having more difficulty.

Embedded Assessment Activities   Assessment activities embedded in each unit will help you examine specific pieces of student work, figure out what they mean, and provide feedback. From the students' point of view, these assessment activities are no different from any others. Each is a learning experience in and of itself, as well as an opportunity for you to gather evidence about students' mathematical understanding.

The embedded assessment activities sometimes involve writing and reflecting; at other times, a discussion or brief interaction between student and teacher; and in still other instances, the creation and explanation of a product. In most cases, the assessments require that students *show* what they did, *write* or *talk* about it, or do both. Having to explain how they worked through a problem helps students be more focused and clear in their mathematical thinking. It also helps them realize that doing mathematics is a process that may involve tentative starts, revising one's approach, taking different paths, and working through ideas.

Teachers often find the hardest part of assessment to be interpreting their students' work. We provide guidelines to help with that interpretation. If you have used a process approach to teaching writing, the assessment in *Investigations* will seem familiar. For many of the assessment activities, a Teacher Note provides examples of student work and a commentary on what it indicates about student thinking.

Documentation of Student Growth

To form an overall picture of mathematical progress, it is important to document each student's work. Many teachers have students keep their work in folders, notebooks, or journals, and some like to have students summarize their learning in journals at the end of each unit. It's important to document students' progress, and we recommend that you keep a portfolio of selected work for each student, unit by unit, for the entire year. The final activity in each *Investigations* unit, called Choosing Student Work to Save, helps you and the students select representative samples for a record of their work.

This kind of regular documentation helps you synthesize information about each student as a mathematical learner. From different pieces of evidence, you can put together the big picture. This synthesis will be invaluable in thinking about where to go next with a particular child, deciding where more work is needed, or explaining to parents (or other teachers) how a child is doing.

If you use portfolios, you need to collect a good balance of work, yet avoid being swamped with an overwhelming amount of paper. Following are some tips for effective portfolios:

- Collect a representative sample of work, including some pieces that students themselves select for inclusion in the portfolio. There should be just a few pieces for each unit, showing different kinds of work—some assignments that involve writing as well as some that do not.

- If students do not date their work, do so yourself so that you can reconstruct the order in which pieces were done.

- Include your reflections on the work. When you are looking back over the whole year, such comments are reminders of what seemed especially interesting about a particular piece; they can also be helpful to other teachers and to parents. Older students should be encouraged to write their own reflections about their work.

Assessment Overview

There are two places to turn for a preview of the assessment opportunities in each *Investigations* unit. The Assessment Resources column in the unit Overview Chart identifies the Teacher Checkpoints and Assessment activities embedded in each investigation, guidelines for observing the students that appear within classroom activities, and any Teacher Notes and Dialogue Boxes that explain what to look for and what types of student responses you might expect to see in your classroom. Additionally, the section About the Assessment in This Unit gives you a detailed list of questions for each investigation, keyed to the mathematical emphases, to help you observe student growth.

Depending on your situation, you may want to provide additional assessment opportunities. Most of the investigations lend themselves to more frequent assessment, simply by having students do more writing and recording while they are working.

Measurement Benchmarks

Content of This Unit In this unit students work with metric and U.S. standard measures of length, distance, weight, and volume, and with measures of time. Throughout the unit, students find and use *benchmarks*. Benchmarks are familiar things that serve as a reference for particular units of measure—for example, two dollar bills placed end to end is about one foot; a fifth grader's little finger is about one centimeter wide; a can of kidney beans weighs about one pound.

Students estimate measurements, and they take actual measurements with metersticks, balance scales, liter measures, and other measuring tools. They also compare their estimates with actual measurements; they compare the sizes of measurement units in different systems; they calculate with measurements; and they investigate ways that people use measurement in their everyday lives.

Connections with Other Units If you are doing the full-year *Investigations* curriculum in the suggested sequence for grade 5, this is the sixth of nine units. Activities with decimals in the Fractions, Percents, and Decimals unit, *Name That Portion,* will be helpful to students in making sense of the metric system of measurement. Your class will have further experience with measuring solid and liquid volume in the 3-D Geometry unit, *Containers and Cubes.*

This unit can also be used successfully at grade 6, depending on the previous experience and needs of your students.

Investigations Curriculum ■ Suggested Grade 5 Sequence

Mathematical Thinking at Grade 5 (Introduction and Landmarks in the Number System)

Picturing Polygons (2-D Geometry)

Name That Portion (Fractions, Percents, and Decimals)

Between Never and Always (Probability)

Building on Numbers You Know (Computation and Estimation Strategies)

▶ *Measurement Benchmarks* (Estimating and Measuring)

Patterns of Change (Tables and Graphs)

Containers and Cubes (3-D Geometry: Volume)

Data: Kids, Cats, and Ads (Statistics)

Investigation 1 ▪ Measures of Length and Distance

Class Sessions	Activities	Pacing
Session 1 (p. 4) EXPLORING MEASUREMENT	Using Tools to Measure Discussion: Two Measurement Systems Homework: Collecting Data	minimum 1 hr
Session 2 (p. 12) USING LENGTH BENCHMARKS	What's a Benchmark? Estimating Lengths with Benchmarks Listing Units of Length and Distance Thinking About How People Measure Homework: When and How Do You Measure?	minimum 1 hr
Session 3 (p. 19) USING MEASURING TOOLS	Reading Measuring Tools Teacher Checkpoint: Measuring Lengths How We Use Measurement Homework: How Tall Is an Adult? Extension: Making Problems	minimum 1 hr
Session 4 (p. 24) MEASURING AND COMPARING	Two Measuring Tasks Why Are Our Measures Different? Guidelines for Measuring Homework: Sharing Measurement Data Extension: How Long Is Our School?	minimum 1 hr
Sessions 5 and 6 (p. 30) MAPPING 100 METERS	How Long Is 100 Meters? Assessment: Measuring in Meters Sharing Our Paths Homework: Should the U.S. Go Metric? Extensions: Walking a Kilometer; Should the U.S. Convert to Metric?	minimum 2 hr
Sessions 7 and 8 (Excursion)* (p. 38) HOW FAR DO PRODUCTS TRAVEL?	Using a Map Scale How Far Away? Sharing What We Discovered Homework: How Far Away? Extensions: Where Were You Born?; News Travels, Too; Manufacturing Centers; The Global Economy	minimum 2 hr

◖ **Ten-Minute Math** ▪ **Estimation and Number Sense**

*Excursions can be omitted without harming the integrity or continuity of the unit, but offer good mathematical work if you have time to include them.

Mathematical Emphasis

- Using U.S. standard and metric tools for measuring length, weight, volume, and time

- Finding and using benchmarks to estimate measures

- Determining when precise measurement is required and when estimates are good enough

- Recognizing and explaining possible sources of measurement error

- Comparing lengths expressed in different ways, such as meters and centimeters, meters and decimal fractions of a meter, and meters and fractions of a meter

- Keeping track of and calculating total measurements

Assessment Resources

Observing the Students (p. 7)

Metric Use Worldwide (Teacher Note, p. 9)

Metric and U.S. Standard Measures (Teacher Note, p. 10)

Introducing Benchmarks (Teacher Note, p. 18)

Teacher Checkpoint: Measuring Lengths (p. 20)

Making Careful Measurements (Teacher Note, p. 23)

Expressing and Comparing Metric Measurements (Teacher Note, p. 28)

Why Do Our Measurements Differ? (Dialogue Box, p. 29)

Assessment: Measuring in Meters (p. 32)

How We Measured 100 Meters (Dialogue Box, p. 37)

Materials

Length, time, weight, and volume measuring tools

Empty containers; trays

Water, sand, rice, or small beans

Chart paper

Scissors

Adding machine tape

Chalk

U.S. and world maps with scales

Stick-on notes

Products with place of origin on label

Overhead projector and pen

Push pins

Calculators

Student Sheets 1–9

Family letter

Investigation 2 ▪ Measures of Weight and Liquid Volume

Class Sessions	Activities	Pacing
Sessions 1 and 2 (p. 46) GROCERY PACKAGE CONTENTS	Measurements on Grocery Labels A Closer Look at Measures of Weight A Closer Look at Liquid Measures Ordering Our Products Homework: How Much . . . ; Vegetable Weights	minimum 2 hr
Session 3 (p. 54) WORKING WITH UNITS OF WEIGHT	Discussion: Units of Weight Making and Comparing Weights Homework: Things I Know About a Kilogram Extension: How Much Do You Carry Home?	minimum 1 hr
Session 4 (p. 58) WORKING WITH UNITS OF LIQUID VOLUME	Measuring Capacity Comparing Liquid Quantities Homework: Things I Know About a Liter Extension: Estimating Liquid Amounts	minimum 1 hr
Session 5 (p. 62) COMPARING WEIGHT AND QUANTITY	Thinking About Density Teacher Checkpoint: Same or Different Weights? Homework: Feathers or Bricks? Extension: Comparing to the Density of Water	minimum 1 hr
Session 6 (p. 66) WRITING ABOUT WEIGHT AND LIQUID MEASURE	Assessment: Describing the Measure of Weight and Liquid Quantity Homework: Vegetable Weights	minimum 1 hr

Sessions 7 and 8 (Excursion)* (p. 68)
ORDINARY AND AMAZING
VEGETABLES
	Organizing Data About Vegetables
	Revealing the Vegetable Record-Breakers
	Comparing Ordinary Vegetables to
	    the Record-Breakers
	Benchmarks for the Record-Breakers
	Homework: Making Record-Breaker Benchmarks
	Extensions: Adding Record-Breakers to the Graphs;
	    Which Is the Most/Least Expensive?
		minimum
		2 hr

◕ **Ten-Minute Math** ▪ **Guess My Unit**

*Excursions can be omitted without harming the integrity or continuity of the unit, but offer good mathematical work if you have time to include them.

Mathematical Emphasis

- Comparing the relative sizes of U.S. standard and metric measures of weight and liquid quantity

- Developing a sense of various weights and developing benchmarks for these measures

- Measuring weight with a balance scale and weights

- Developing a sense of various volumes and developing benchmarks for these measures

- Developing meaning for the concepts of volume and density; distinguishing between quantity and weight

Assessment Resources

Volume, Capacity, and the Measure of Liquids (Teacher Note, p. 52)

Ordering Our Products by Metric Weights (Dialogue Box, p. 53)

Observing the Students (p. 59)

Teacher Checkpoint: Same or Different Weights? (p. 63)

Learning to Distinguish Between Quantity and Weight (Teacher Note, p. 65)

Assessment: Describing the Measure of Weight and Liquid Quantity (p. 66)

Observing the Students (p. 70)

Observing the Students (p. 71)

Sketch Graphs: Quick to Make, Easy to Read (Teacher Note, p. 73)

Materials

Overhead projector

Cans, packages, or bottles labeled by weight and liquid quantity

Balances or scales; weights

Paper or plastic bags

Materials that vary in density

Stick-on notes or masking tape

Liquid measuring tools

Empty containers; trays

Water, vegetables, oil, sand

Chart paper

Calculators

Student Sheets 10–19

Teaching resource sheets

Investigation 3 ▪ It's About Time

Class Sessions	Activities	Pacing
Session 1 (p. 76) ESTIMATING HALF A MINUTE	Discussion: Units of Time Reading the Second Hand Estimating 30 Seconds Graphing the Estimates Homework: Commercial Minutes Extension: Summarizing Data	minimum 1 hr
Session 2 (p. 81) COMMERCIAL MINUTES	Commercials: Analyzing the Data Discussion: How Much TV Do We Watch? Assessment: A Year's Worth of Commercials Homework: Adults' Ages Extensions: Hours and Hours of Commercials; Benchmarks for Other Units of Time	minimum 1 hr
Session 3 (p. 87) MAKING SENSE OF YEARS	How Many Times as Old? How Much Older? Lifetime Strips Choosing Student Work to Save Homework: Comparing Ages Extensions: Making Historical Strips; Moving from Strips to Calculators; Representing a Millennium	minimum 1 hr

◔ **Ten-Minute Math** ▪ **Guess My Unit**

Mathematical Emphasis	Assessment Resources	Materials
▪ Developing vocabulary for units of time ▪ Developing benchmarks for minutes and for years ▪ Timing in minutes and seconds ▪ Collecting, displaying, and analyzing data ▪ Using measurement conversions (minutes to hours to days) in the problem-solving process ▪ Keeping track of computations in a multistep problem	Assessment: A Year's Worth of Commercials (p. 82) The Shape of the Data: Clumps, Bumps, and Holes (Teacher Note, p. 84) Finding the Typical Number of Commercial Minutes (Dialogue Box, p. 85) Assessment: A Year's Worth of Commercials (Teacher Note, p. 86) Choosing Student Work to Save (p. 90)	Clock or watch with a second hand Calculators Overhead projector Scissors Tape Chart paper Construction paper Student Sheets 20–23 Teaching resource sheets

Following are the basic materials needed for the activities in this unit. Many of the items can be purchased from the publisher, either individually or in the Teacher Resource Package and the Student Materials Kit for grade 5. Detailed information is available on the *Investigations* order form. To obtain this form, call toll-free 1-800-872-1100 and ask for a Dale Seymour customer service representative.

For Measuring Length

Metersticks or metric measuring tapes: 1 per pair of students

Foot rulers marked with centimeters: 1 per pair of students

Maps, U.S. and world, with scale: 1 per 4 students

Products with place of origin on label: 1 per student. Students may bring these from home.

For Measuring Weight

Balances or scales that measure up to 1.5 kilograms: 3 or 4 per class

Metric weights—1 kilogram, 500 grams, 100 grams: 3 sets per class. **Note:** One standard set is included in the kit. More can be purchased, or you can easily make inexpensive sets using containers of pennies or metal washers.

U.S. standard weights—1 pound, 1 ounce: 4 sets per class. (You might use a 1-pound box of sugar as a pound weight, and 10 pennies as 1 ounce.)

Cans, packages, or bottles labeled by weight: 1 per pair. Students may bring these from home.

Materials that vary in density and shape, such as foam, scrap paper, gravel, small wood scraps or shavings, sponges, pennies, nails, centimeter cubes, marbles, interlocking cubes, paper clips, or wooden blocks

Paper or plastic bags: 10–12 small, 16–18 large

For Measuring Liquids

Liter measures marked in milliliters: 4 per class

Quart and cup measures: 4 per class

1-fluid-ounce measures: 4 per class, optional

Water, sand, rice, or small beans

Trays to catch spills: at least 2 per class

Containers of various sizes: 15–20 per class

Full or empty cans, packages, or bottles labeled by volume: 1 per pair. Students may bring these from home.

Three identical transparent plastic containers, one filled with water, one with vegetable oil, and one with sand

For Measuring Time

Watches or large clock with a second hand

Other Supplies

Scissors: 1 per pair of students

Calculators: at least 1 per pair of students

Adding machine tape: 1 roll

Chalk

Tape

Stick-on notes: 2–3 small pads to share, or masking tape

Large chart or poster paper: several sheets per group

Construction paper

Overhead projector

Paper and pencils

The following materials are provided at the end of this unit as blackline masters. A Student Activity Booklet containing all student sheets and teaching resources needed for individual work is available.

Family Letter (p. 100)

Student Sheets 1–23 (p. 101)

Teaching Resources:

   One-Centimeter Graph Paper (p. 124)

   Guess My Unit Cards (p. 125)

Practice Pages (p. 127)

Related Children's Literature

Dahl, Roald. *Esio Trot*. New York: Puffin Books, 1990.

Juster, Norton. *The Phantom Tollbooth*. New York: Random House, 1961.

Milton, Nancy. *The Giraffe That Walked to Paris*. New York: Crown Publishers, 1992.

In this unit, students come to understand metric and U.S. standard measures of length, distance, weight, and liquid volume, and common measures of time.

Although students in the upper elementary grades hear and read about measurement information all the time, they often have little sense of the actual sizes of measurement units. In a social studies book, for example, they might read that a certain river is 100 meters wide, but have no sense of how big that is. Is that a little stream you could leap across? a very wide river you could barely see across? Is it wider than the classroom? wider than the school?

One way for students to develop a good understanding of measures is by finding and using *benchmarks*. A benchmark is something familiar that is about the same size as a given unit of measure. Benchmarks help us understand and compare units of measure, help us estimate size, and help us interpret measurement information. For example, if the students find that their little finger is about a centimeter wide, they can use that finger to estimate the length of something in centimeters. If students know that their classroom is about 10 meters long, they can use that image to comprehend the length of a dinosaur described in a book as 11.5 meters from head to tail.

To find their own benchmarks during this unit, students actively measure many things. They use rulers and metersticks to find length and distance, a balance to determine weight, a liter measure to determine liquid volume, and clocks or watches to measure time. As students learn about using different measurement tools, they become aware of common measurement errors and how to correct them. They also come to understand the importance of measuring correctly, and they develop a sense of when a measurement seems about right and when it seems too large or too small and needs to be checked.

As students work with benchmarks, they consider the degree of precision required by different measurement situations. When is a student's height from floor to shoulder—measuring 93 centimeters—a good benchmark for a meter? When is a more precise benchmark necessary? In what situations would an accurate measurement with a meterstick be required?

Throughout the unit, students work with number and computation. They compare equivalent measurements expressed in different forms (for example, kilograms and grams, as well as kilograms and fractions or decimal fractions of a kilogram). They explore the relationships between units in different measurement systems (which is greater, a fluid ounce or a milliliter?) and within measurement systems (how many milliliters in a liter?). They analyze measurement data they have gathered (what is the shortest measurement our class got for the length of the classroom? the longest measurement? a typical measurement?).

Note: This unit does not include activities that involve *area* or *temperature*. There are no special tools for measuring area, a two-dimensional measure; students work with the concept of area in the 2-D and 3-D geometry units for grade 5. If you want to introduce the measure of temperature during this unit or later in the year, see the **Teacher Note**, Metric and U.S. Standard Measures (p. 10), for some ideas.

At the beginning of each investigation, the Mathematical Emphasis section tells you what is most important for students to learn about during that investigation. Many of these mathematical understandings and processes are difficult and complex. Students gradually learn more and more about each idea over many years of schooling. Individual students will begin and end the unit with different levels of knowledge and skill, but all will gain some facility with units of measurement and will develop strategies for estimating measures and using measurement tools to achieve greater accuracy.

Throughout the *Investigations* curriculum, there are many opportunities for ongoing daily assessment as you observe, listen to, and interact with students at work. In this unit, you will find two Teacher Checkpoints:

> Investigation 1, Session 3:
> Measuring Lengths (p. 20)

> Investigation 2, Session 5:
> Same or Different Weights? (p. 63)

This unit also has two embedded assessment activities:

> Investigation 1, Sessions 5–6:
> Measuring in Meters (p. 32)

> Investigation 2, Session 6:
> Describing the Measure of Weight and Liquid Quantity (p. 66)

In addition, you can use almost any activity in this unit to assess your students' needs and strengths. Listed below are questions to help you focus your observation in each investigation. You may want to keep track of your observations for each student to help you plan your curriculum and monitor students' growth. Suggestions for documenting student growth can be found in the section About Assessment.

Investigation 1: Measures of Length and Distance

- How do students use U.S. standard and metric tools to measure length, weight, volume, and time? How accurate are their measurements? How effectively do they incorporate suggestions for alternative ways of using the tools? How do students keep track of and calculate total measurements?

- How do students go about finding and using familiar benchmarks to estimate measures? What experiences do students use to generate meaningful benchmarks? How do they use these benchmarks to help estimate size?

- How do students decide if a precise measurement is required or if an estimate is good enough?

- How independently do students recognize measurement error? How do they explain possible sources of the error?

- How do students make sense of and use relationships among units in the metric system? How do they compare lengths expressed in different ways (such as meters and centimeters, meters and decimal fractions of a meter, and meters and fractions of a meter)?

- What strategies do students use to keep track of and calculate total measurements?

Investigation 2: Measures of Weight and Liquid Volume

- How do students compare the relative sizes of U.S. standard and metric measures of weight and liquid quantity? How easily do they move back and forth between measures? How do they use a balance scale to investigate and prove relationships among units?

- How developed is students' sense of the relative measures of weight: 1 kilogram, 500 grams, 100 grams, 1 gram, 1 pound, and 1 ounce? Have they developed appropriate benchmarks for these measures? How do they use them?

- How do students measure weight with a balance scale and weights (both metric and U.S. standard)? How accurate are their measurements?

- How developed is students' sense of the relative measures of liquid volume: 1 liter, 500 milliliters, 1 milliliter, 1 quart, 1 cup, and 1 fluid ounce? Have they developed appropriate benchmarks for these measures? How do they use them?

- How do students make sense of volume? Do they think of volume as the amount of space something takes up, or the amount a container can hold?

- How do students make sense of density? of differences between quantity and weight? How do they estimate the relative weights of and amounts in a set of containers?

Investigation 3: It's About Time

- How do students talk about units of time? What terminology do they use?

- How do students find and use benchmarks for minutes and years? What experiences do students use to develop benchmarks meaningful to them?

- How comfortable and accurate are students in timing minutes and seconds?

- How do students go about collecting, displaying, and analyzing data? How do they keep track of their data? How do they choose to represent the data? Do their representations and interpretations highlight important features of the data (such as clumps of data, holes in the data, outliers)?

- How do students solve problems that involve measurement conversions (minutes to hours to days)? What strategies do they use?

- How do students keep track of computations in a multistep problem?

In the *Investigations* curriculum, mathematical vocabulary is introduced naturally during the activities. We don't ask students to learn definitions of new terms; rather, they come to understand such words as *factor* or *area* or *symmetry* by hearing them used frequently in discussion as they investigate new concepts. This approach is compatible with current theories of second-language acquisition, which emphasize the use of new vocabulary in meaningful contexts while students are actively involved with objects, pictures, and physical movement.

Listed below are some key words used in this unit that will not be new to most English speakers at this age level, but may be unfamiliar to students with limited English proficiency. You will want to spend additional time working on these words with your students who are learning English. If your students are working with a second-language teacher, you might enlist your colleague's aid in familiarizing students with these words, before and during this unit. In the classroom, look for opportunities for students to hear and use these words. Activities you can use to present the words are given in the appendix, Vocabulary Support for Second-Language Learners (p. 97).

scale, pound, weight, weighs   In the opening activity and then throughout Investigation 2, students use a balance scale as they look for weight benchmarks and measure the weight of different items.

estimate, exact, precise   Students see that we can use benchmarks to estimate measures, while we use tools to make exact measurements when precision is needed.

personal   Students find that some benchmarks will work for everyone, but that others—such as the length of one's own foot—are *personal* benchmarks that may work only for a single person.

product, bottle, can, box, containers   A close look at grocery products in various containers gives students a real-world sense of the use of measures of weight and liquid volume.

space   Volume—liquid or dry—is seen as the amount of space something takes up.

liquid   Students see that liquid is measured by units of liquid volume—fluid ounces, cups, and quarts, or liters and milliliters.

Multicultural Extensions for All Students

Whenever possible, encourage students to share words, objects, customs, or any aspects of daily life from their own cultures and backgrounds that are relevant to the activities in this unit. For example, students can bring in measuring tools that their families use. Cookbooks from countries that use the metric system may list ingredients in grams; clothing or shoes may be sized in centimeters.

Investigations

INVESTIGATION 1

Measures of Length and Distance

What Happens

Session 1: Exploring Measurement Students rotate among four measurement centers: at the *length* center they find objects that are about a foot, about a meter, and about a centimeter long; at the *time* center they find something that takes about a minute to do; at the *weight* center they find things that weigh about a pound and about a kilogram; and at the *liquid quantity* center they find things that hold about a liter and about a cup. They decide as a group which measurement units are from the U.S. standard system and which are from the metric system.

Session 2: Using Length Benchmarks Students learn about the use of *benchmarks* to estimate measures. They list some of the benchmarks they found in Session 1 and others they are familiar with. They use their benchmarks to estimate lengths, and they discuss other units of length and distance.

Session 3: Using Measuring Tools Students examine scales on metersticks and foot rulers to become more familiar with the tools and to compare units. They measure the lengths they previously estimated with benchmarks. As a class, they list situations in which estimates of length are sufficient and situations in which accurate measurements are required.

Session 4: Measuring and Comparing Student pairs work on two measuring tasks: They make a strip of paper as tall as an adult, and they remeasure the strip to find the height in a different measurement system (if they began with U.S. standard units, they measure the strip in metric, and vice versa). They also measure the length of the classroom in meters, and they consider why some students came up with different measurements.

Sessions 5 and 6: Mapping 100 Meters As a way of understanding how far 100 meters is, students measure and mark out a path 100 meters long. They make maps showing their 100-meter paths. As an assessment, students individually demonstrate how they would make an accurate measurement in meters.

Sessions 7 and 8 (Excursion): How Far Do Products Travel? Students investigate how far different products travel to get to their city or town. Using the places of origin given on product labels, they use a map scale to determine the distance each product has come. Students pool their findings to investigate the data further.

Mathematical Emphasis

- Using tools for measuring length, weight, volume, and time
- Recognizing which measurement units are U.S. standard and which are metric
- Recognizing uses of benchmarks to estimate
- Deciding when precise measurement is required and when estimates are good enough
- Recognizing and explaining possible sources of measurement error
- Comparing lengths expressed in different ways, such as meters and centimeters, meters and decimal fractions of a meter, and meters and fractions of a meter
- Keeping track of and calculating total measurements
- Developing benchmarks for 100 meters
- Measuring distances of 100 meters
- Comparing distances expressed in hundreds or thousands of miles or kilometers
- Using scale on maps to calculate approximate distances

What to Plan Ahead of Time

Materials

- Metersticks or metric measuring tapes: 1 per pair (Sessions 1, 3–6)
- Foot rulers marked with centimeters: 1 per pair (Sessions 1, 3–4, 7–8)
- Watches with second hands: 4. These are needed only if there is no large class clock that shows seconds. (Session 1)
- Pan balances: 2 (Session 1)
- 1-kilogram weights (could use containers of pennies or metal washers): 2 (Session 1)
- 1-pound weights (could use 1-pound box of sugar): 2 (Session 1)
- Liter measures marked in milliliters: 2 (Session 1)
- Cup measures: 2 (Session 1)
- Empty containers of various sizes: 10–15 (Session 1). One of these should hold close to 1 liter and another close to 1 cup.
- Water, sand, rice, or small beans (Session 1)
- Trays to catch spills: 2 (Session 1)
- Chart paper (Sessions 1–2, 4, 7–8)
- Scissors: 1 per pair (Session 4)
- Push pins: 4 per student (Session 3)
- Adding machine tape: 1 roll (Sessions 4–6)
- Chalk: 1 piece per group (Sessions 5–6)
- U.S. and world maps with scales: 1 per 4 students (Sessions 7–8, Excursion)
- Stick-on notes: 1 pad per 4 students (Sessions 7–8, Excursion)
- Products with place of origin on label: 1 per student (Sessions 7–8, Excursion)
- Overhead projector and pen (Sessions 5–6, 7–8, Excursion)
- Calculators (Sessions 5–6)

Other Preparation

- Set up four measuring centers before starting Session 1 (see p. 5).
- Duplicate student sheets and teaching resources (located at the end of this unit) in the following quantities. If you have Student Activity Booklets, copy only the item marked with an asterisk.

For Session 1
Student Sheet 1, Exploring Measurement (p. 101): 1 per student

For Session 2
Family letter* (p. 100): 1 per student. Remember to sign it before copying.

Student Sheet 2, Benchmark Estimates (p. 102): 1 per student

Student Sheet 3, When and How Do You Measure? (p. 103): 1 per student (homework)

For Session 3
Student Sheet 4, How Tall Is an Adult? (p. 104): 1 per student (homework)

For Session 4
Student Sheet 5, Explaining Measurement Differences (p. 105): 1 per student

Student Sheet 6, Sharing Measurement Data (p. 106): 1 per student (homework)

For Sessions 5–6
Student Sheet 7, Should the U.S. Go Metric? (p. 107): 1 per student (homework)

For Sessions 7–8 (Excursion)
Student Sheet 8, How Far Products Travel (p. 108): 1 per student, plus 1 transparency*

Student Sheet 9, How Far Away? (p. 109): 1 per student (homework)

Exploring Measurement

Materials

- Metersticks and foot rulers (2 of each)
- Watches that show seconds (4) or class clock with a second hand
- Pan balances (2)
- Kilogram and pound weights (2 of each)
- Liter and cup measures (2 of each)
- Empty containers of various sizes (10–15)
- Water, sand, rice, or small beans
- Trays to catch spills (2)
- Student Sheet 1 (1 per student)
- Folders for student work (1 per student, optional)
- Chart paper (optional)

What Happens

Students rotate among four measurement centers: at the *length* center they find objects that are about a foot, about a meter, and about a centimeter long; at the *time* center they find something that takes about a minute to do; at the *weight* center they find things that weigh about a pound and about a kilogram; and at the *liquid quantity* center they find things that hold about a liter and about a cup. They decide as a group which measurement units are from the U.S. standard system and which are from the metric system. Their work focuses on:

- using tools to measure length, weight, liquid quantity, and duration of time
- finding benchmarks for foot, meter, minute, pound, kilogram, liter, and cup
- identifying units as either metric or U.S. standard

Using Tools to Measure

Four Measuring Centers Although most of Investigation 1 focuses specifically on measures of length and distance, students begin their study of measurement with an activity that gives them an overview of the tools and techniques they will be using throughout the unit for measuring length, time, weight, and liquid quantity. For most of Session 1, pairs of students will be working simultaneously at four measuring centers around the classroom.

How to Set Up the Centers For each center, set apart an area where from two to four pairs of students can be working at the same time. Label each center as appropriate: Length, Time, Weight, Liquid Quantity. The requirements for the four centers are as follows:

> Center 1: Length—2 metersticks, 2 foot rulers marked with centimeters
>
> Center 2: Time—4 watches (analog or digital) that show seconds—or if there is a large class clock with a second hand, set up this center near the clock
>
> Center 3: Weight—2 pan balances, 2 one-kilogram weights, 2 one-pound weights (could be one-pound boxes of sugar)
>
> Center 4: Liquid Quantity—2 liter measures marked in milliliters, 2 one-cup measures, 10–15 empty containers of various sizes, ample amounts of a pourable substance (water, sand, rice, or small beans), 2 trays to catch spills

Introducing the Measuring Centers Distribute Student Sheet 1, Exploring Measurement, to each student. Explain what materials are at each measuring center, and point out that the student sheet tells what to do at the different centers.

Assure students that they do not need to find something that is exactly the same as each of the units. For example, we might say that something 11 inches or 13 inches is "about" as long as a foot. It is up to students to decide how close they want to get to the actual measurement.

Students work in pairs, spending about 10 minutes on each measuring activity. Explain the order in which students will rotate among the measuring centers. Several pairs can work at a center at the same time, depending on the number of tools and the space available.

Center 1: Length

Students use a meterstick to find something about as long as a meter; they use a ruler to find something that is about as long as a foot; and they may use either the ruler or meterstick to find something about as long as a centimeter. These can be lengths on their own bodies. They record a description of the objects they find, using pictures or words.

Center 2: Time

Students use a clock or watch that shows seconds to find something that takes close to one minute to do. They might try doing something repeatedly, so that, for example, they might find the number of times they can snap their fingers in a minute. Or they might find a particular activity that takes about one minute, such as going to the pencil sharpener, sharpening a pencil, and returning to their seats. Again, they describe their findings using pictures or words.

Center 3: Weight

Students use a kilogram weight and a balance to find something that weighs about as much as a kilogram. Students put the kilogram weight in one pan of the balance and find an object or combination of objects that they can place in the other pan to balance it. They do the same with a pound. Using words or pictures, they record a description of the objects they find.

Some students may have had little past experience working with balances. In many cases, objects of the same weight will not appear to "balance" unless they are placed at equal distances from the fulcrum. That is, an object placed in the pan so that it sits closer to the fulcrum will seem relatively lighter than an object placed further away. If your classroom balances are sensitive to this, students may discover while they are working that they can make something balance the given weight by moving it to a different part of the pan. If you observe this, discuss students' experiences with seesaws. Ask if they have ever tried to balance two children of different weights on a seesaw by adjusting their distance from the fulcrum. Explore with students how to get a "true" balance by placing the objects at equal distances from the fulcrum.

Be sure students understand that to balance the scale, they will add or remove objects from the pan, *not* adjust the distance of the objects from the fulcrum.

Center 4: Liquid Quantity

Students use water, sand, or another pourable substance and a liter measure marked in milliliters to find something that holds about a liter. Students fill the liter measure and then find a container, such as a bucket, vase, or bottle, that is full when holding the same amount of material. They do the same with a cup. They record a description (verbal or pictorial) of the objects they find.

Observing the Students

Circulate among the centers to observe students' use of tools. If students seem uncertain of how to use a particular tool, encourage them to puzzle things through and to help one another. When you see a tool being used incorrectly, suggest an alternative way to use it and ask if that would work.

As you circulate, check that students are recording clear descriptions of their findings, so that someone else reading the description would know exactly what they meant—for example, a careful description such as "Two social studies books and a paperback mystery weigh about a kilogram" is preferable to the less specific "Three books weigh about a kilogram." Remind students that they can draw pictures to help show what they find.

Discussion: Two Measurement Systems

List on the board or on chart paper the units of measure students have been using at the centers: meter, foot, centimeter, minute, kilogram, pound, liter, cup.

We use two systems of measurement in the United States. Sometimes we use the U.S. standard system. Other times we use the metric system. At the measuring centers, you used units from both systems. Do you know which of these are metric units?

Mark the metric units on the list as students agree: meter, centimeter, kilogram, liter.

Has anyone been in a country that uses _only_ the metric system? What units did you see used? What were they used for? Have you noticed metric units being used in the United States? How are they used?

Invite students to share their experiences with metric measure. Also, talk with students about the advantages and the problems of converting to the metric system, as discussed in the **Teacher Note**, Metric Use Worldwide (p. 9).

While many students may be familiar with meters and centimeters from measuring with these units in school, don't expect them to know the difference between metric and U.S. standard measures for weight and liquid quantity. They may be familiar with liters and quarts from containers for soft drinks and milk, yet not realize that these units come from two different measuring systems.

Some students who have lived in other countries will be familiar with metric measures for weight and liquid quantity. The cooks in their families may use a metric scale with grams and kilograms instead of measuring cups for dry ingredients, and may have milliliter measures instead of fluid ounces and cups for liquids. For more information about the two systems, see the **Teacher Note**, Metric and U.S. Standard Measures (p. 10). Explain to students that for the next few weeks, they will continue working with units from *both* systems.

Following their work in Session 1, be sure that students keep their completed Student Sheet 1 in a safe place. They will need it during Investigation 2, when they will be referring back to their first measures of weight and liquid quantity. If you plan to have students keep their work for the unit in math folders, distribute them at this time.

Session 1 Follow-Up

🏠 Homework

Collecting Data   If you plan to do the excursion in Sessions 7 and 8, students can begin to collect product containers—cans, boxes, bags—that they will use to investigate the distances products have traveled. The product containers should have labels that indicate the place where the product is made, packaged, or distributed. Show the class a labeled product, perhaps from someone's lunch, and demonstrate finding where the place of origin is printed.

If possible, each student should bring in one container that comes from the United States and one that comes from elsewhere. The containers may be full or empty. If they are full, students may put their names on them and take them home at the end of the unit. Some full containers will be useful in Investigation 2 as well.

Metric Use Worldwide

Only the United States and three or four other countries are not officially metric. In many countries, people are unfamiliar with the U.S. (or English) standard units that we use; they "think" in metric. They buy food by the kilogram and drinks by the liter. They drive kilometers per hour in cars powered with gas bought by the liter. They know their height in centimeters, their weight in kilograms, and the temperature in Celsius. If you asked most Australians how much they weigh in pounds, they would have just as little idea as if you asked most U.S. residents for their weight in kilograms.

In other countries, however, use of the metric system is more piecemeal. In England, where conversion to the metric system has been taking place slowly over the last 30 years, many people are somewhat familiar with both systems. For some kinds of things, people use both metric and standard units. Fruit and vegetables are sold by the pound in some stores but by the kilogram or half kilogram in others. Some food packages are labeled in standard units, some in metric, and some in both. And some cookbooks only use metric units, while others offer both metric and standard versions of the same recipe. For some measures, people use *only* metric, and for others, *only* standard units. For example, school children learn to measure small lengths in centimeters, but may think of their own heights in feet and inches. Temperature is discussed exclusively in Celsius, but road signs give distances in miles, and drinks are sold in pints.

While people in many metric countries use some nonmetric units, overall most of the measuring that goes on in the world is in metric. That means all the products people use in their lives—from bathroom scales to measuring jugs—are labeled in metric. In order not to lose out on export opportunities all over the world, many U.S. industries have begun to manufacture parts and products sized and labeled in metric. Metric units are used in the manufacture of cars, pharmaceuticals, medical equipment, film, cameras, optical equipment, computers, and construction equipment. In many other industries, however, U.S. goods are manufactured with U.S. standard sizes and parts. These need to be relabeled and repackaged if they are sold to people in other countries, just as manufacturers in other countries often need to change their labels and packaging for us.

While many experts believe that the U.S. will have to convert to metric eventually if we are to stay competitive in the world market, there has been a great deal of resistance to conversion because of the cost. Workers will need to be retrained; school curricula will need to change; public education programs will need to be launched to get people to think in metric; and everything from thermometers to road signs will need to be relabeled in metric. But, metric advocates claim, what seems a great cost now will bring us far greater gains in the long run.

Most countries use the metric system, and the increasingly global marketplace has led experts to predict that the United States will soon convert, willingly or not. (See the **Teacher Note**, Metric Use Worldwide, p. 9). Thus we feel strongly that mathematics education should be increasingly based in and on the metric system. However, the reality in this country—where reliance on U.S. standard or English measures is commonplace—requires that we also discuss and include some nonmetric units, including pounds, feet, and miles.

In the metric system, there are many useful relationships among units of measure—something the U.S. standard system lacks. For example, 1 cubic centimeter is equal to 1 milliliter, and 1 milliliter of water weighs 1 gram; 1 liter is 1000 milliliters, and 1 liter of water weighs 1 kilogram. A liter also has the same volume as a cube that is 10 centimeters by 10 centimeters by 10 centimeters. (In base ten blocks, this is the 1000 block.)

The metric system is based on powers of ten. This simplifies calculations and conversions. Prefixes are used across measurement types to denote the magnitude, or power of ten, of the measurement in question. The most common of these are *kilo-, centi-,* and *milli-. Kilo-* means a thousand; therefore, 1000 meters is a *kilometer. Centi-* means one-hundredth, so one-hundredth of a meter is a *centimeter. Milli-* means one-thousandth; a millimeter is one-thousandth of a meter. At each end of the scale are *mega-* and *micro-,* representing one million and one-millionth, respectively. Other metric prefixes, such as *deca-, deci-,* and *hecta-,* are less commonly used.

	Metric System	**U.S. Standard System**
length or distance	meter (abbreviated m) centimeter (0.01 meter) kilometer (1000 meters)	foot (abbreviated ft or ') yard (3 feet) inch (1/12 foot) mile (5280 feet)
liquid volume how much space a liquid occupies	liter (abbreviated l) milliliter (00.001 liter)	fluid ounce (abbreviated fl oz) pint (16 fluid ounces) quart (2 pints or 32 fl oz)
solid volume how much space something takes up	cubic centimeter (abbreviated cc) cubic meter (1,000,000 cc)	cubic inch (abbreviated cu in) cubic foot (1728 cu in) cubic yard (27 cu ft)
weight*	gram (abbreviated g) kilogram (1000 grams) metric ton (1000 kg)	ounce (abbreviated oz) pound (abbreviated lb; 16 oz) ton (2000 pounds)
temperature	0° Celsius (freezing) 100° C (boiling) 20° C (room temperature)	32° Fahrenheit (freezing) 212° F (boiling) 68° F (room temperature)

* In science, the metric units *grams* and *kilograms* are measures of mass, or how much matter there is, whereas the U.S. standard units *ounces* and *pounds* are measures of *weight,* which is the force of Earth's gravity on an object's mass. But in everyday usage and throughout this unit, we use both types of units as measures of *weight.*

Continued on next page

Adults who are accustomed to U.S. standard measures may use them as benchmarks to get a sense of metric units. For example, many of you know that a meter is a little longer than a yard; a kilometer is a little more than half a mile; a liter is a little more than a quart; a kilogram is a little heavier than 2 pounds.

Most of your students will be learning about metric measures through their own experiences as they compare them to common objects. Thus, they might learn:

- A millimeter is about the thickness of a dime or a paper clip wire.

- A centimeter is about the width of a regular paper clip.

- A meter is about the length from the tip of your fingers to your opposite shoulder, the width of an average doorway, or as high as an average kitchen counter.

- The height of a tall man is about 200 centimeters.

- A coffee cup holds about 250 milliliters.

- A gram is about the weight of two regular paper clips or a dime.

- A newborn baby weighs about 3 kilograms.

Temperature Activities for exploring the measurement of temperature are not included in this unit. If you would like to introduce the Celsius and Fahrenheit scales, students might establish benchmark temperatures—"freezing," "comfortable," and "boiling"—by using thermometers to measure the temperature of ice water, room-temperature water, and just-boiled water. The Celsius temperatures of freezing and boiling water are, like other metric measures, easily remembered numbers—although students may not measure exactly 0° C or 100° C, as these are the temperatures of freezing and boiling water under ideal conditions.

Using Length Benchmarks

Materials

- Student Sheet 2 (1 per student)
- Student Sheet 3 (1 per student, homework)
- Chart paper
- Family letter (1 per student)

What Happens

Students learn about the use of *benchmarks* to estimate measures. They list some of the benchmarks they found in Session 1 and others they are familiar with. They use their benchmarks to estimate lengths, and they discuss other units of length and distance. Student work focuses on:

- Recognizing uses of benchmarks to estimate measures
- Recognizing and explaining possible sources of measurement error
- Listing measures of length and distance

 Ten-Minute Math: Estimation and Number Sense Three or four times during the next two weeks, try the Ten-Minute Math activity Estimation and Number Sense. These activities are designed to be done in any 10 minutes outside of math class, perhaps before lunch or at the end of the day.

In this activity, students mentally estimate an answer to a problem that you show for a brief time. Then they see the problem again and find a more precise solution.

Show each problem on the board or overhead for 10 to 15 seconds (or longer when you are first introducing the activity). Then cover the problem. Ask students what they noticed, and how they might do the problem in their heads. Uncover the problem and allow another 10 seconds or so for students to consider it further. In a follow-up discussion, students share the ways they came up with a reasonable estimate or an accurate answer to the problem.

Do two or three similar problems in a session. You might start with addition and subtraction problems like these:

$26 + 49 + 75 =$	$38 - 15 + 17 + 10 =$	$100 - 68 =$
$35 + 6 - 15 =$	$52 - 4 - 7 + 27 + 4 =$	$102 - 54 =$
$100 + 6 - 50 =$	$20 - 100 - 18 + 500 =$	$134 - 95 =$

At other Ten-Minute Math times or for homework, students can make up their own problems to challenge the class. Encourage them to set up an addition or subtraction problem with several parts, first in an order that is easy to compute mentally (e.g., $75 + 24 + 7$), and then in an order that is more difficult (e.g., $24 + 7 + 75$).

For variations on this activity, see p. 93.

Use students' work at the measuring centers in the previous session to introduce the use of *benchmarks* for various units of measure. See the **Teacher Note**, Introducing Benchmarks (p. 18), for further suggestions.

Make a two-column chart on a piece or half piece of chart paper. Title the chart *Measures of Length and Distance.* Label one column *Units* and the other *Benchmarks.* In the units column, write *foot, meter,* and *centimeter,* leaving enough space to allow for more than one benchmark for each unit.

Yesterday at the measuring centers you used tools to find things that are about the same as particular units of measurement—things about as long as a foot, about as heavy as a pound, and so on. We're going to talk about how you could use some of these things to help you estimate lengths.

Suppose you had a spool of ribbon and you needed to cut a ribbon about two feet long, but you didn't have a foot ruler or a yardstick. Is there something you could use instead?

As students suggest ideas for ways to estimate the length of something in feet, remind them to consider the objects they found at the length measuring center.

❖ **Tip for the Linguistically Diverse Classroom** Turn this discussion into a hands-on activity. Using a spool of ribbon, challenge student volunteers to demonstrate their ideas of using benchmarks to estimate a piece of ribbon two feet long.

The things we can use to help us estimate length are called *benchmarks*. A benchmark is something familiar that is the same size—or almost the same size—as a unit of measure. Benchmarks can help you get a sense of just how big these units are.

Some benchmarks that students suggest will work for everyone in the class—for example, a sheet of standard notebook paper is about a foot long. Students may also suggest "personal" benchmarks that will not work for everyone. A personal benchmark has special meaning for just one person. For example, if your foot is close to a foot long, then that's a good personal benchmark for you, but it would not work for someone whose feet are much smaller than yours. On the chart, write two or three suggested benchmarks for a foot that would be useful to most of the class.

Collect two or three ideas for benchmarks for a meter and a centimeter and add them to the chart.

What's a Benchmark?

Measures of Length and Distance	
Units	Benchmarks

Spend a little time talking about the possible benchmarks for other measures (time, weight, and liquid quantity) that students identified at the centers.

At the measuring centers, you found some benchmarks for other measurement units. What did you find that would make a good benchmark for a pound?

Can you think of other things you might find at home or in a store that are about as heavy as a pound? About as long as a foot?

As needed, remind students that benchmarks don't need to be *exactly* equal to the measurement unit, just close. At this point in the unit, there may not be many additional suggestions.

In the next few weeks, we'll be finding more benchmarks for a foot, a meter, a kilogram, a pound, and other measurement units.

Students might keep their own benchmark lists as they work through this unit, including both class benchmarks (from the chart) and their personal benchmarks.

Post the Measures of Length and Distance chart in a convenient place where students may add to it later in this investigation and refer to it throughout the measurement unit.

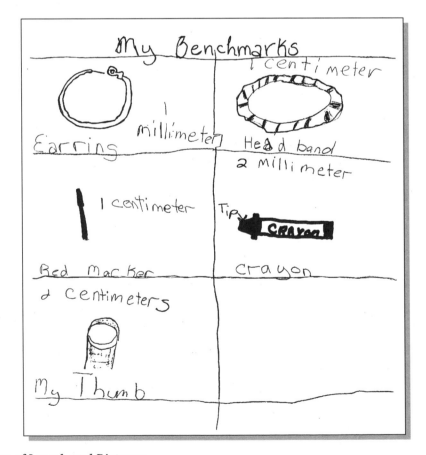

Estimating Lengths with Benchmarks

Record on the board a few lengths that students can estimate from or near their seats. These lengths should span a range of sizes so that students may use different benchmarks. For example:

Use your benchmarks to estimate these.

1. the width of your pencil
2. the width of your desk
3. the height of your desk
4. the length of your notebook
5. the width of a classroom window
6. your own height

Distribute Student Sheet 2, Benchmark Estimates, to each student. (Do not distribute any measuring tools for this estimation activity; the students will use tools in the next session.) Students work in pairs to estimate each of the lengths listed on the board. First, the pair decides which unit they will use to make a particular estimate. Then, each student chooses a benchmark for that unit to estimate the length of the object. Both students record a description of the object and its estimated size—both their own and their partner's estimate.

❖ **Tip for the Linguistically Diverse Classroom** Pair second-language learners with English-proficient students for this task. Partners include simple drawings of each object they list in the first column on Student Sheet 2.

Assure students that it is fine to come up with different estimates; in fact, it is expected. They discuss with their partner why their estimates differ (when they do), and then write a note about it in the third column on the student sheet, *Why estimates differ.* They might also write where they predict the actual measurement (which they will be making in the next session) will fall—in between the two estimates, a bit longer than either estimate, or a bit shorter.

Students may find that some benchmarks are easier to use than others for making certain kinds of estimates. For example, using a forearm as a benchmark for 1 foot may work well for estimating desk width, but would be awkward for estimating the desk's height. If you notice any students having such difficulty with a particular benchmark, suggest that they choose a different one.

Comparing Estimates When everyone has finished estimating the length of the listed items, call the class together briefly to share how they chose a unit and made their estimates.

Did you and your partner ever get different estimates for the same thing? Why do you think this happened?

Ask for a few volunteers to explain why they think their estimates were not the same as their partner's. Possible explanations include using benchmarks that are not the same size (for example, one person might have used a benchmark that is a little more than a meter, and another might have used a benchmark that is a little less than a meter), and using different strategies for approximating an estimate to the nearest unit or part of a unit.

Remind students to put Student Sheet 2 in a safe place, because they will be filling in the last column in the next session.

Activity

Listing Units of Length and Distance

Keep this discussion very brief, leaving time at the end of the session to introduce the homework. Draw attention to the chart you started at the beginning of this session.

So far, we have been using feet, meters, and centimeters to measure how long things are, or how far it is from one point to another. What are some other measures of length and distance?

Record students' suggestions in the *Units* column. Encourage them to include metric units by asking them about any you think they will be familiar with, such as the metric unit to measure long distances (kilometer), or the smallest metric unit on a classroom ruler (millimeter, or one-tenth of a centimeter). Students may notice that the same measurement units can be used for length, width, height, depth, and longer distances.

Do you have benchmarks for any of these new units? Which of the units on this list can you imagine? Which can you estimate the size of?

Record on the chart any appropriate benchmarks that students suggest. Assure the class that they will have more chances to develop benchmarks for length and distance measures over the next couple of weeks.

❖ **Tip for the Linguistically Diverse Classroom** Include on the chart simple drawings to identify each benchmark that students suggest.

Thinking About How People Measure

Get students started thinking about practical, everyday uses of measuring.

Outside of school, how do people use measurement? Think about the people at home or in your neighborhood. What kinds of things do they measure? How do they do it?

Do they use measuring tools? Do they use benchmarks to estimate how much or how big?

Sometimes people use informal measures—like *handfuls* when they cook. A *handful* is not a benchmark for a particular unit of measure, but it is a personal measure. That is, a handful of flour will be about the same every time the same person uses that much.

People use other informal, personal measures: Have you ever seen any-one estimate lengths with their hand span? Or with an arm length? Or a pace?

After this discussion, explain the homework (see below). Students will use the results of this homework for discussion in the next class session.

Session 2 Follow-Up

When and How Do You Measure?   Send home the family letter, or the *Investigations* at Home booklet, and Student Sheet 3, When and How Do You Measure? Using the questions on Student Sheet 3 to guide them, students talk to one or more adults to find at least three situations in which they measure.

Students should look for two kinds of situations: those in which people measure with tools (a tape measure for a construction job, a measuring cup for baking), and those in which they use estimated amounts (a pinch of salt in cooking, or a trowel of dirt in planting). Remind students to bring Student Sheet 3 to class tomorrow.

❖ **Tip for the Linguistically Diverse Classroom** Students with limited English proficiency can answer the questions with drawings of people using measuring tools or estimated amounts.

A benchmark is something familiar that is about the same size as a particular unit of measurement. We can use benchmarks to help estimate the size of something when a measuring tool is not handy. For example, if we know that the nail of our index finger is about a centimeter wide, we can use it to estimate length in centimeters. We can also use benchmarks to help us understand and remember the size of a measurement unit.

When introducing benchmarks to the class, encourage students to share ways that measurement units have become meaningful to them. In one class, the teacher began by telling a story about a benchmark of her own:

"When I was a little girl, I lived in a house that was on top of a hill. My mother was a wonderful cook. She loved to bake. A lot of times, she'd be in the middle of baking and she would run out of an ingredient. She used to send me to the store for 5-pound bags of sugar or flour. If I think back to walking up that hill with that bag, I have a memory of what 5 pounds feels like. So now whenever somebody tells me that something weighs around 5 pounds, I remember what it felt like to carry those 5-pound bags of sugar up that hill."

After the teacher told her story, she invited other students to share their own stories about familiar benchmarks. Several students shared ways that they found meaning for a mile:

Manuel: When you walk a mile, it takes about half an hour. When my mom and I run together on Saturdays, we go four times around the track to make a mile. I don't know how long it takes, but I get really tired!

Lindsay: I like watching the odometer in the car when my parents drive. Sometimes I time how long it takes to go a mile. It takes about a minute when we're on the highway, but sometimes when we're in traffic it takes a minute and a half or two minutes or even longer.

Shakita: It's a mile to downtown from school. I know because I bike downtown to my flute lesson after school every Thursday.

Noah: I used to live in New York City, and there a wide city block is about a tenth of a mile, so when you walk ten blocks across town, you go a mile. And when you walk on the short blocks going up and down it takes twenty blocks to go a mile.

The more that students can bring their out-of-school experiences into math class, the more meaningful and engaging learning will be. As students share the ways that they have come to develop their own benchmarks, they develop new insights about the meaning of measurement units.

Using Measuring Tools

What Happens

Students examine scales on metersticks and foot rulers to become more familiar with the tools and to compare units. They measure the lengths they previously estimated with benchmarks. As a class, they list situations in which estimates of length are sufficient and situations in which accurate measurements are required. Student work focuses on:

- becoming familiar with scales on foot rulers and metersticks or tapes
- measuring with rulers and metersticks or tapes
- deciding when precise measurement is required and when estimates are good enough

Materials

- Metersticks or tapes (1 per pair)
- Foot rulers (1 per pair)
- Each student's Benchmark Estimates (Student Sheet 2), partially completed in previous session
- Students' completed Student Sheet 3
- Student Sheet 4 (1 per student, homework)
- Scissors
- Push pins (4 per student)

Activity

Reading Measuring Tools

Distribute foot rulers and metersticks or tapes to pairs of students. Review with them how to read measuring tools.

Can you find a millimeter? a centimeter? a foot? Can you use your meterstick to show how many millimeters in a centimeter? how many centimeters in a meter?

Some students will need help differentiating between metric and standard measuring tools (or between the metric and standard sides of a tool with units marked on both sides). If you have a combination tool and also have separate metric and standard measuring tools for students to use, it may be helpful to tape over the entire standard side of the meterstick. Some students will also need help identifying the marks for centimeters and for millimeters.

Write the following questions on the board:

> Which is larger, an inch or a centimeter?
> Which is larger, a meter or a yard?
> How many millimeters between the 1 and the 2 on the meterstick?
> How many millimeters between the 47 and the 49 on the meterstick?
> How many centimeters between the 47 and the 49 on the meterstick?
> What does the 90 on the meterstick mean? Is that more or less than a meter?
> How many centimeters in a meter?

Students take a few minutes to find the answers with a partner.

❖ **Tip for the Linguistically Diverse Classroom** Pair second-language learners with English-proficient students. Instruct the English-proficient students to read aloud each question on the board to their partner as they address it.

Ask for a few volunteers to give their answers and explain how they know.

Activity

Teacher Checkpoint

Measuring Lengths

Students now measure the lengths they estimated in the previous session for Student Sheet 2, Benchmark Estimates. They measure with the same units they used to make their estimates, and they record their measurements in the last column. If partners come up with different measurements, they record both.

Students may need reassurance that it's perfectly OK if their measurements are not the same as their estimates. Using benchmarks to estimate is a skill that takes a lot of practice. They should not expect to be estimation experts yet.

As students work, use this as a checkpoint. Circulate to observe them using measuring tools and recording their measurements. You may decide to take time to review correct measurement practices with individuals, pairs, or with the whole class. Consider the following:

- Can the student read the calibrations on the measuring tool correctly?
- Does the student know not to mix metric and standard units when taking a measurement?
- Does the student position the measuring tool to get the most accurate measurement?

- Does the student position the measuring tool correctly when moving it repeatedly to measure a longer length?
- How does the student approximate the final portion of the measurement?
- How does the student keep track of and calculate the total measurement?
- Does the student consider whether the total measurement is reasonable, and if necessary, check it?

The **Teacher Note**, Making Careful Measurements (p. 23), provides additional information on skills and understandings students need in order to measure carefully.

How We Use Measurement

Direct students to cut out the boxes for each measurement situation they recorded on Student Sheet 3 for homework in Session 2. On a bulletin board or the wall, place two titles: *Exact Measures* and *Estimated Measures*. Here students can post the results of their interviews.

When you interviewed people about the times when they measure, what did you find out? When do they try to measure exactly? When do they estimate?

After students post each of their interview responses under the appropriate title, discuss the different situations. Students who have forgotten to bring in any responses may add them to the display over the next day or two.

Exact Measures | Estimated Measures

look at the odometer in the car to see how far we have gone

mom uses a gauge to see if there is enough air in the tires

My aunt lines up the edge of the cloth with a little nick on her sewing machine to get the right seam width.

use arm lengths to see if a piece of furniture will fit in a space along a wall.

My mother uses a tape measure to find the size of mats and frames and prints for framing pictures

fever thermometer to measure your temperature

measure out shampoo in your hand

Dad walks off distances to estimate the size of a room or a rug or a garden. (His foot is about a foot long.)

What are the advantages of exact measures in some of these situations? What are the advantages of estimated measures?

After discussing the adults' uses of measurement, students spend a few minutes at the end of the session thinking about their own use of measurement.

When are estimates of length good enough? When would you need a precise measurement?

They might look over their Student Sheet 2, Benchmark Estimates, to think about the estimates and measures they recorded for lengths and distances in the classroom. Students might consider, for example, the width of a classroom window. If they were growing plants for a science experiment and wanted to determine about how many plants would fit on each windowsill, an estimate of window width would be good enough. If they were getting dimensions for new window shades, on the other hand, a precise measurement would be needed.

Session 3 Follow-Up

🏠 Homework

How Tall Is an Adult?   For use in the Session 4 activities, students ask an adult outside of class for his or her height and record the information on Student Sheet 4, How Tall Is an Adult? They can record the heights either in feet and inches or in centimeters. Remind students to bring Student Sheet 4 to class tomorrow.

📐 Extension

Making Problems   Students might make up mental addition and subtraction problems for use in Ten-Minute Math, Estimation and Number Sense activities, as described on p. 12. Ask them to write two versions of each problem: one with the numbers arranged to make the problem appear difficult, and one arranged so it looks easier. For example, they might present $45 - 8 - 5 + 9$, which could be rearranged to $45 - 5 + 9 - 8$.

Students can make their problems as complicated as they want, using many numbers or using decimals or fractions. For example:

$$\tfrac{3}{4} + \tfrac{2}{3} + 1\tfrac{1}{4} + \tfrac{4}{3}$$

Whatever the problem, they must be able to show it in an "easy" version and be able to do it themselves.

Making Careful Measurements

In the upper elementary grades, many students have little experience actually taking measurements. Those who have done sewing or woodworking are more likely to be able to measure correctly. They may also have a better sense of when a measurement is "about right" and when it needs to be checked. To measure accurately, students need both mechanical skills and conceptual understandings. Techniques that are important for careful measuring include the following:

- lining up the measuring tool exactly at 0 when beginning a new measurement, and reading the calibrations on the measuring tool correctly

- working either in meters and centimeters or feet and inches—but not a mixture of metric and standard systems

- positioning the measuring tool against the object being measured

- measuring from the same end of the measuring tool with each repeated use when measuring a large distance

- accurately approximating the final portion of the measurement

- keeping track of partial measures and calculating the total measurement

Conceptual understandings that are important include these:

- knowing *why* these measuring techniques are important—for example, why metric and standard units should not be combined in measurements

- recognizing when precise measurement is needed, and when it is not

- knowing how to determine if a measurement is reasonable or if it is necessary to check it

As students work on measurement activities, circulate through the class to observe. This way, you can help them learn the skill of measuring while they are actually doing it. You can also discuss with students the reasonableness of their measurements, help them explore possible sources of measurement error, and encourage them to check and revise measurements as needed.

Measuring and Comparing

Materials

- Metersticks or tapes (1 per pair)
- Foot rulers (1 per pair)
- Adding machine tape (1 roll)
- Scissors (1 per pair)
- Students' completed Student Sheet 4
- Student Sheet 5 (1 per student)
- Student Sheet 6 (1 per student, homework)
- Masking Tape (optional)
- Chart paper

What Happens

Student pairs work on two measuring tasks: They make a strip of paper as tall as an adult, and they remeasure the strip to find the height in a different measurement system (if they began with U.S. standard units, they measure the strip in metric, and vice versa). They also measure the length of the classroom in meters, and they consider why some students came up with different measurements. Student work focuses on:

- recognizing and explaining possible sources of measurement error
- comparing lengths expressed in different ways, such as meters and centimeters, meters and decimal fractions of a meter, and meters and fractions of a meter
- keeping track of and calculating total measurements

Activity

Two Measuring Tasks

Distribute the materials and introduce the two tasks as explained below. Note that for the second task, it is easier to get accurate measurements (for the length of the classroom) if only a small number of students work on this task at the same time. Thus, as students begin work on the paper strip task, call up one or two pairs to measure the length of the classroom. When they are finished, they may return to the paper strip task while another pair or two measures the length of the classroom.

Task 1: Making Paper Strips for Adult Heights   Students will need to refer to the adult's height they recorded on Student Sheet 4 for Session 3 homework. Each of them will use the adding machine tape to make a strip of paper as tall as that adult. Partners will check one another's measurements before cutting their strips. Next, students measure their strip with different units. If they cut the strip based on a measure in feet and inches, they measure it in centimeters this time; if they cut it based on centimeters, they now measure it in feet and inches. They label each strip at the bottom with the name of the adult and the measurement, both in feet and inches and in centimeters.

Note: If your students are using a combination measuring tool—metersticks marked with feet and inches on one side—remind them to use the metric side when measuring in centimeters and the U.S. standard side when measuring in feet and inches. You might tape off the section of the inches side from 36 inches to the end, explaining to students that the untaped portion is exactly three feet.

If you have available space, students can post their strips in the classroom. Help them post the strips with the bottom flush with the floor.

Task 2: Measuring Our Classroom   Introduce the second task by explaining exactly what students are to measure. Your directions, of course, will depend on the size, shape, and layout of your classroom. Following are some guidelines to consider in setting up the task:

- If the length is along a wall, clearly mark the start and end points. You may choose a length that has one or two small obstructions, such as a small bookcase or radiator. Students will need to find ways to measure around the obstructions or to estimate the length of the portion of the wall that is obstructed.

- If you do not have a long wall, or if your walls have many obstructions, you might run a strip of masking tape on the floor across the length or width of the classroom for students to measure. Or, you might ask students to measure the length of the classroom along the corridor *outside* the room, if start and end points can be made clear.

- If you have a large class, you might ask some pairs to measure the *width* of the classroom and others to measure the *length*. Make sure that at least six pairs measure each dimension, since students will later be considering why some pairs got different measurements when they measured the same thing.

- If measuring the room itself is too difficult, choose a straight length on the floor that is several meters long, so that students need to pick up and put down a meterstick or tape several times in order to measure the entire length.

When you have explained what students are to measure, gather a few quick estimates of the length of this dimension in meters and record them on the board.

Students may use metersticks or short measuring tapes to measure the length of the classroom. As one student measures, the other checks that the measuring is done carefully. Students record their results.

As students work on the two tasks, circulate to observe them using measuring tools once more before you assess their measuring skills in Sessions 5 and 6. Use these observations to help focus on good measurement practices during the class discussion, Guidelines for Measuring, later in this session.

Students who finish early can write about how they made sure they measured accurately.

Why Are Our Measures Different?

After everyone has measured the classroom, gather the class together to share their measurements and their strategies for making them.

❖ **Tip for the Linguistically Diverse Classroom**   Partners with limited English proficiency can demonstrate how they got their measurements.

Record on the board each pair's measurement, and briefly compare the actual measurements to estimates made before the students began measuring. Discuss briefly why different pairs might have gotten different measurements. See the **Dialogue Box**, Why Do Our Measurements Differ? (p. 29), for part of such a discussion.

Sometimes the difference will arise from how students approximated the final portion of the measurement. Possible strategies include approximating to the next largest or next smallest centimeter, approximating to the nearest five or ten centimeters, and approximating to the nearest quarter or half meter.

Distribute Student Sheet 5, Explaining Measurement Differences. Students continue to work in the same pairs, discussing answers with their partners, but writing answers on their own sheets. They record all the measurements the class came up with, and they propose possible reasons for getting one of the *smaller* and one of the *larger* measurements. If different pairs measured different dimensions of the room, students record and write about only the measurements for the dimension they measured.

As students work, circulate to make sure they can compare measurements to identify one of the smaller and one of the larger measurements. See the **Teacher Note**, Expressing and Comparing Metric Measurements (p. 28), for ways you might assist students who are having difficulty.

Possible reasons for getting a larger measurement include placing the meterstick or tape incorrectly on subsequent measures so that meters overlap; approximating the measurement to the next largest meter; placing the meterstick or tape so that it zigzags across the wall or floor; or making mistakes in calculating the total measurement. Possible reasons for getting a smaller measurement include underestimating distance if a portion of the wall cannot be directly measured; not keeping track of all the meters measured; placing the meterstick or tape incorrectly so that there is a gap between meters measured; or leaving off the final portion of a meter left at the end of the measurement.

Students who finish early can write about what they think the actual length of the classroom is, and why.

Guidelines for Measuring

What are some things to remember when you're measuring? What are some tips you might give someone else who is learning to measure with a meterstick or a ruler?

Work with the students to create a class chart of guidelines for measuring. As students suggest good measurement practices and explain why each is important, record their ideas on a chart. One class came up with the following chart:

> Guidelines for measuring
> — Don't mix metric and standard units.
> — Hold the ruler straight against the thing you are measuring.
> — Mark where the ruler ends with your finger, then move it and start it at your finger. Could use pencil instead of finger.
> — Make sure you start measuring at 0.
> — Write down each time you put the ruler down so you don't lose track.

❖ **Tip for the Linguistically Diverse Classroom** Ask for volunteers to illustrate each measuring guideline listed on the class chart.

Session 4 Follow-Up

Sharing Measurement Data Send home Student Sheet 6, Sharing Measurement Data, and the paper strip students used to represent the height of the adult they measured. Student Sheet 6 consists of two parts. First, students report on the results of the paper-strip task to the adult whose height they worked with. If adults gave their height in feet and inches, students tell them their height in centimeters, and vice versa. Second, students list any benchmarks they use for an inch, a foot, a yard, a centimeter, and a meter in the table on Student Sheet 6.

 **Homework**

How Long Is Our School? Using the length of their classroom as a benchmark, students estimate the length and perhaps the width of the school. They make sketches of the floor plan of the school and show how they made their estimates.

 **Extension**

Expressing and Comparing Metric Measurements

In this unit, students make and record many metric measurements. Some students will find it natural to express their measurements as a whole number of units and a fractional part (2 and ¼ meters); some will express their measurements as a whole number of units and a decimal part (2.25 meters); some will express their measurements as a number of larger units and a number of smaller units (2 meters and 25 centimeters); and some will express their measurements as a number of smaller units (225 centimeters).

Rather than insisting on a uniform way of expressing metric measurements, you can use the variety of expressions that students offer as a springboard for exploring topics such as finding equivalent ways to express the same measurement, comparing measurements, and finding relationships among fractions and decimals.

Throughout the unit, ask questions such as the following:

■ **How else could you say it?** When recording measurements on the board, stop occasionally to ask if anyone knows a different way to express the measurement. For example, in one class, when a student reported that she had measured the width of a door and found it to be 1 meter and 6 centimeters, the teacher asked the class to suggest other ways of expressing the same measurement. She recorded each of the students' suggestions:

> 1 meter and 6 centimeters
> about 1 meter
> 1.06 meters
> 1 and 6/100 meters
> 1 and 3/50 meters
> 106 centimeters

■ **How do you know the expressions are equivalent?** Encourage students to explain how they know. The student who suggested 1 and 6/100 centimeters explained that she knew "0.06 is the same as six one hundredths." The student who suggested 1 and 3/50 said that he knew that 3/50 is equal to 6/100 because 6 is half of 3 and 50 is half of 100. And, the student who offered "about 1 meter" explained that 6 centimeters is only a very small part of a meter.

■ **Which is larger?** If you have recorded several different measurements on the board, ask students to find the largest and smallest. If students have difficulty comparing measurements expressed in different ways, suggest they find another way to express some of the measurements so that they will be easier to compare. For example, if students do not know how to compare 10½ meters to 10 meters and 350 centimeters, they might write ten and ½ meters as 10.5 meters, 1,050 centimeters, or 10 meters and 500 centimeters—which they can more easily compare to 10 meters and 350 centimeters. Similarly, a student who is having difficulty telling whether 1.06 meters is larger than 1.2 meters might "convert" both measurements to centimeters, perhaps with the help of a meterstick, to find out.

If finding different ways to express and compare metric measures becomes a natural part of class sharing and discussion, students will strengthen their understanding of relationships among units in the metric system, and they will come to appreciate that the metric system makes it easy to express parts of units with decimals and to convert from one unit to another.

Why Do Our Measurements Differ?

In this discussion, students suggest reasons why their measures of the same classroom dimension might have differed. Sometimes they find it difficult to decide if what they did would result in a larger or smaller number of meters.

Sofia, why did you say our measurements might be different?

Sofia: Well, one reason is they probably measured a different length. Maybe it was smaller or bigger.

Corey: But we all measured the same part of the room.

Sofia: But maybe someone measured it crooked or something. Then it would seem smaller.

Trevor: I think it would be bigger. On a zigzag path you walk further. I think it would work that way here.

Sofia: Oh yeah. A straight across line would be smaller. A crooked line would be bigger.

Robby: Maybe they used something different to measure.

Jasmine: Yeah, like maybe they used their benchmark and it was bigger. Then you get smaller measurements. Or if your benchmark was too small then you'll get bigger ones.

Matt: Maybe people did not measure accurately.

What does that mean for you, Matt? How did you make sure that you measured accurately?

Matt: We held it [the meterstick] straight.

Marcus: And we marked it with a pencil.

Alani: And then we put our finger down and moved it and started it at my finger.

Julie: Maybe some people put it slanted. Or maybe they lost their place.

Jeff: Well first we tried holding it [the meterstick] in the air and going across, but we couldn't hold it straight so we had to do it on the floor.

Cara: We thought we did ours right, but then we looked at everyone else's and ours was way off and we couldn't figure out why. Then Ms. Novo helped us figure it out. We had a meterstick but it only went to 90 centimeters.

Tai: We did that too! When we started first, we had a yardstick but thought it was a meterstick.

Leon: Well we used one of those meter strings and it got all stretched around things in our way. But then shouldn't ours [measurement] be bigger?

Alani: Not if you really stretched it. Then you made it reach further, and you didn't need to do the string so many times.

Mapping 100 Meters

Materials

- Metersticks or metric tape (1 per small group)
- Calculators
- Chalk (1 piece per group)
- Adding machine tape (optional, several meters per group)
- Student Sheet 7 (1 per student, homework)
- Overhead projector (optional)

What Happens

As a way of understanding how far 100 meters is, students measure and mark out a path 100 meters long. They make maps showing their 100-meter paths. As an assessment, students individually demonstrate how they would make an accurate measurement in meters. Student work focuses on:

- developing benchmarks for 100 meters
- measuring distances of 100 meters

 Ten-Minute Math: Estimation and Number Sense Use any free 10 minutes during the day, outside of math class, to continue work with Estimation and Number Sense.

Pose more addition and subtraction problems, perhaps problems with fractions or decimals. Begin with problems with two addends, and proceed to more difficult problems like those below. Ask students what *whole number* the answer is near, or what two whole numbers the answer is between.

$\frac{1}{2} + \frac{1}{3} + \frac{3}{6} =$	$\frac{5}{10} + \frac{8}{4} + \frac{3}{3} =$	$8 - 0.7 + 0.2 =$
$\frac{2}{3} + \frac{1}{3} + \frac{4}{8} =$	$\frac{12}{6} + \frac{1}{12} + \frac{12}{4} =$	$32.04 + 8 + 5.7 =$
$\frac{3}{4} + \frac{3}{3} + \frac{5}{4} =$	$0.4 + 8 + 0.6 =$	$1.1 - 0.2 + 0.5 =$

For full instructions and variations, see p. 93.

Activity

How Long Is 100 Meters?

Today, we'll be making some paths that are about 100 meters long. We found out that our classroom is about ___ meters long. About how many times as long as our classroom is 100 meters?

Students might figure this out individually or with a neighbor. Ask a few students to share their strategies. Possible strategies include these:

- Approximate the length of the room to the nearest meter and use repeated addition ("It's about nine times as long, because the room is about 11 meters long, and if you add 11 nine times, you get 99").

- Approximate the length of the room to the nearest meter and use knowledge of multiplication facts ("The room is about 12 meters long. We knew 12×8 is 96 and 12×9 is 108. So it's a little more than 8 times as long").
- Mentally or with a calculator, divide 100 by the length of the room.

Ask students to try to picture a distance of 100 meters in their minds.

What might be a benchmark for 100 meters? Do you think the school hallway is about 100 meters long? the front of the school building? the parking lot? the school yard? If you go out the front door of the school and walk for 100 meters, where do you think you'll be?

Some students may find it helpful to use the length of the classroom as a basis for estimating distances. For example, if 100 meters is about nine times as long as the classroom, they might try to imagine a path that is about nine times as long as their classroom.

Ask a few students to share their thinking with the class.

Planning the 100-Meter Path   For this activity, the directions you give will depend on the layout of your school and grounds and the safety of the area around your school. You will need to decide if it is best to measure 100 meters within the school, outside, or beyond the school grounds. The more flexibility you can provide, the more opportunities students will have to develop a range of 100-meter benchmarks. If possible, the paths should extend in a straight line from the starting point to the ending point, or be a loop that does not repeat the same path.

After you have explained *where* students may take their measurements, form small groups of three or four students to plan how to make a 100-meter path. Students will need to make several decisions. You might list these on the board or overhead as reminders:

- **Where will the path begin?**   Students might decide to begin the path on the sidewalk outside of school, at one end of the school yard, or at one end of a corridor in the school.
- **How will you measure the path?**   Students may use one-meter lengths of adding machine tape, their benchmarks, metersticks, or metric measuring tapes. They could also measure out a length of paper tape that is longer than a meter—say, 10 meters—to use as a measuring tool. Students will have to figure out how many times they need to put down the tape in order to measure out 100 meters.

Note: String or yarn is *not* a good measuring tool for this activity, because it can stretch considerably when used for making repeated measurements.

■ **How will you mark the path?**   If the path is to be on pavement, students may be able to mark its start, end, and entire length with chalk. If it is to be on grass, they will need to find some other way of marking at least the start and end points of the path.

In a brief conference with each group, make sure they have their plans worked out and their materials ready. Also see that students have made plans to keep records and mark off distances as they go along. There is nothing more frustrating for students than getting toward the end of this task and realizing they've lost track of the count.

Measuring the Path   Decide when students will do the actual measuring. They might do it during class time, during recess, or after school. Small groups may need to work at different times in order to avoid collisions between groups in the chosen location.

After measuring, each student records individually what the group used as a measuring tool, the length of their measuring tool, and the number of times they needed to lay down the measuring tool to measure 100 meters. Each student also sketches a full-page map showing where the group measured 100 meters. The map should clearly show the start and end points of the path.

Activity

Assessment

Measuring in Meters

As students work on their maps, call up students individually to take a measurement in meters. Ask them to measure something that requires repeated use of the measuring tool, such as the width of the chalkboard. Ask students to tell you the answer and to write it down.

As each student works, observe the following:

■ Can the student read the calibrations on the measuring tool correctly?

■ Does the student use metric and only metric units?

■ Does the student position the measuring tool to get the most accurate measurement?

■ Can the student correctly position the tool for repeated placement?

■ How does the student approximate the final portion of the measurement?

■ How does the student keep track of and calculate the total measurement?

■ Does the student consider whether the total measurement is reasonable, and, if necessary, double-check it?

Spend several minutes with each student. You might also ask questions that require reasoning about or comparing measurements. For example:

■ One person measured the length of the chalkboard and got 2½ meters. Another measured the same board and got 2.4 meters. Which measure is larger? How do you know? Why do you think one person might have come up with a larger measurement than another?

■ Why do we take measurements only in metric or only in U.S. standard units? Why not mix the two systems?

If you do not have time to assess each student during this session, continue the process over the next couple of days during math class, or at another time when students are working quietly at their seats.

Sharing Our Paths

Follow up the 100-meter path activity with small-group presentations. Each group shares a map of their path and their strategies for measuring. Depending on the size and layout of your class and the time you have available, you might organize the presentations in one of the following ways:

■ Each group presents to the whole class for 2–3 minutes. Each group member has a task: one tells why they chose the area they did; one tells how they measured; one shows a map; and one tells of any surprises they had about how "long" or "short" their paths are.

■ Divide the groups into the Presenters and the Visitors. Each Presenter group sets up at a particular center in the classroom and displays their map. The Visitors rotate among the centers, spending a minute or two at each. The Presenters tell each Visitor group why they chose the area they did and how they measured. The Visitors may ask questions to make sure they understand exactly how the Presenters determined their path. When all the Visitor groups have visited all the Presenter groups, switch roles and repeat the activity.

See the **Dialogue Box**, How We Measured 100 Meters (p. 37), for some strategies students used to plan a 100-meter path.

If some of the 100-meter paths are especially memorable, students may want to add them to the class benchmarks list or to their own lists of personal benchmarks.

How Long Is a Kilometer?   To help students become familiar with the length of a kilometer, we highly recommend the Walking a Kilometer extension (p. 36). This involves establishing a kilometer walk near the school and walking it with the students, keeping track of the time it takes.

Whether or not you are able to take this kilometer walk, hold a brief discussion of kilometers.

In the metric system, people use *kilometers* to measure large distances. A kilometer is 1000 meters.

How many times would you need to walk the 100-meter path you just made to walk a kilometer?

How long do you think it would take to walk a kilometer at a normal pace—ten times the length of the 100-meter path you found?

Sessions 5 and 6 Follow-Up

Should the U.S. Go Metric?   Assign Student Sheet 7, Should the U.S. Go Metric?, at the end of Session 5 and allow students two nights to complete it. Students ask an adult the following questions:

> Do you think it makes sense for the United States to convert to metric? Why or why not?

They record the adult's responses, perhaps in the form of a brief newspaper article with a list of pros and cons.

❖ **Tip for the Linguistically Diverse Classroom**   Students may use their primary language to interview adults and record responses.

Reminder   If you are doing the excursion in Sessions 7 and 8, How Far Do Products Travel?, remind students about bringing in one or two product containers. The containers should have labels that indicate specifically where the product is made or packaged. If possible, each student should bring in one container that comes from the United States and one that comes from another country. For this activity, containers can be empty; however, if they are full, they can be saved and used again for Investigation 2.

Preparation   For use in Investigation 2, students need to bring from home two grocery items. Each student should try to bring one package, can, or bottle with the *weight* of the contents labeled, and one with the *liquid volume* of the contents labeled. *The item labeled by weight must be full. The item labeled by liquid volume can be full or empty.*

Remind students to ask their parents if they may bring these items to school for a few days; everything can be returned. (See bottom of Student Sheet 7.) Plan to have extras available if anyone cannot bring something in. Students should write their names on anything they plan to take back home.

Show students where to find weight or liquid volume listed on a couple of items so they will know what to look for. Explain that the capacity of containers—how much they hold—is given in many different ways. Some packages will give net weights in pounds (lb) or ounces (oz) alone; others will also list the weight in grams (g).

Packages that contain fluids—beverages, sauces, cooking oils, shampoo, dishwashing liquid—will give fluid volume in liters (l) and milliliters (ml), quarts (qt) and pints (pt), or fluid ounces (fl oz) instead of weight.

Be aware of the confusion that can arise in U.S. standard measure because the unit *ounces* is used in two different ways: *ounces* that are measures of weight, and *fluid ounces* that are measures of liquid volume. Suggest that students look closely for these two different types of units on the packages they bring in.

Extensions

Walking a Kilometer Plan a kilometer walk (just over 0.6 mile) near the school, perhaps out to a place that is a half kilometer from the school and back. Use a city map or a car odometer (you may need to convert miles to kilometers) to plan your walk.

Make a simple map of the area that includes the walk, showing intersections and other landmarks. You should mark the starting point of the walk, but not the end point. Distribute copies of this map. Tell students what road or street route you will be walking. Students mark the place on the map where they estimate the kilometer (or half kilometer) will end and estimate the time it will take them to walk it.

Even if you agree as a class that everyone will walk at a normal speed, some will walk faster than others. Be sure that the adult walking with the lead group knows where the kilometer ends. Students are to time the walk at their own pace. Once they have this personal experience with the length of a kilometer, students may want to add a brief description of the kilometer path to the class list of length benchmarks.

Should the U.S. Convert to Metric? Some students may be interested in organizing a class debate on whether the United States should convert entirely to the metric system. In order to prepare for the debate, both sides should consider questions like these: What are the advantages of converting? What are the disadvantages? What kinds of things would need to change? (products, school books, scales in stores and doctor's offices, car and bicycle speedometers, etc.) How long might it take people to learn to "think" in metric?

❖ **Tip for the Linguistically Diverse Classroom** Pair second-language learners with English-proficient students as debate partners. Those with limited English proficiency can provide the visuals to be used in the debate (for example, a poster labeled *Advantages,* showing drawings of the partners' ideas).

How We Measured 100 Meters

As these students were sharing their 100-meter paths with the class (p. 33), they described a number of strategies for measuring 100 meters:

Becky: We laid out a measuring tape to find out how many of my feet are in a meter. I walked toe to heel and it was 4 of my feet for a meter. Then I started walking at home plate. When we got to 400 we knew it was 100 meters. We got to right before the basketball court, so from home plate to right before the basketball court is 100 meters.

Amir: We did the fence along the side of the school yard. We measured and found out that each fence post is 3 meters apart. We knew that the closest number to 100 we could get to by 3's is 99. Then we did 3 into 99 and got 33. So it's 33 fence posts and then one-third more because one-third of 3 is 1, and 99 and 1 is 100. So if you start at the entrance to the school yard, 100 meters along the fence is near that dark pile of dirt.

Desiree: We decided to just do 50. Five of my feet is a meter, and Jessica counted 1, 2, 3, 4, 5. She wrote the number every time I stepped 5 times until she got to 50. I started at the door by the cafeteria and got to almost the end of the parking lot, so we figured that almost to the end of the parking lot and back would be 100 meters.

Noah: We started at the dirt island behind the school. We used a broom handle to measure 100 meters from the island. The broom handle was 120 centimeters long, so we added broom handles until we got to 10,000 centimeters. That's the same as 100 meters. We got to the beginning of the field where we play softball.

Maricel: We came in late from band practice so we didn't get a chance to measure, but we figured out that it's down the hall and then back again as far as the big bulletin board. When we measured the classroom a few days ago, it was about 12 meters long. So, we figured it is about 60 meters to the end of the hall. There's our room, that's 12 meters, then Ms. Sanchez's room—24 meters, then Mr. Yung's—36, Ms. Hegarty's—48, and Ms. Zollo's at the end makes 60. Then, if you come back, it's 72 to go past Ms. Zollo's again, 84 to go past Ms. Hegarty's, 96 to the end of Mr. Yung's. The bulletin board is about halfway between Mr. Yung's door and Ms. Sanchez's door, so that's about 100 meters.

How Far Do Products Travel?

Materials

- Foot rulers (1 per group)
- Product containers with place of origin on label (at least 1 per student)
- U.S. and world maps with scales (1 of each per group)
- Stick-on notes (1 pad per group)
- Student Sheet 8 (1 per student, plus transparency)
- Overhead projector and pen
- Atlas (optional)
- Student Sheet 9 (1 per student, homework)
- Chart paper (optional)

What Happens

Students investigate how far different products travel to get to their city or town. They begin by using product labels to find where the products are from. After locating these places of origin on a U.S. or world map, they determine the distance each product has traveled, and they identify the products that have traveled the shortest and longest distances. Students pool their findings to investigate the data further. Student work focuses on:

- comparing distances expressed in hundreds or thousands of miles or kilometers
- using scale on maps to calculate approximate distances

Activity

Using a Map Scale

For this activity, the students work in groups of four. Students who are familiar with map scales might be grouped with those who have had little or no experience with reading maps and using the scale.

Distribute the maps and rulers to each group. Give students time to become familiar with their maps. Ask them to locate a few places on each map, including their hometowns.

The amount of introduction needed will depend on your students' prior experience with scale on maps. Students who have worked with the *Investigations* grade 4 unit, *Money, Miles, and Large Numbers,* will have used a scale to determine distances on a map.

Who knows what a map scale is? What does it show? What do we use a map scale for?

What is the scale on our U.S. map? What does the scale tell us?

As needed, offer an explanation of scale:

When people are using a map, they often want to know how far it is from one place to another. On a map, the scale helps you find that out. On this U.S. map, for example, [1 inch] stands for [150 miles]. *[Substitute the correct information from the map you are using.]*

Help students locate the scale on their map, and write the scale information on the board.

In your group, use your map to find out about how far away Chicago *[or substitute a familiar city on your U.S. map]* **is from here. You may use your rulers to figure out the distance on the map, or you may use a strip of paper that matches the size of the scale.**

When students have finished, they share strategies and results with the class. Possible strategies include calculating the distance 1 inch at a time— that is, the first inch represents 150 miles; the second another 150 miles, which makes it 300; the next inch is another 150 miles, which is 450; and so on. Or, students might measure the distance in inches and multiply that measure by the number of miles each inch represents.

If answers in the class vary, ask students to suggest why this might be so. Rounding measurements or making slight errors in measurement can result in very different distances. Assure students that for most purposes, when using this type of map, they only need to find out "about" how far away places are. Their estimates should be close to the actual distances, but do not need to be exact.

What is the scale of your world map?

Write the scale information for the world map on the board.

Can you find Cairo, Egypt *[or substitute a city shown on your world map],* **on this map?**

Once students have located Cairo, they use the scale to find out about how far away it is from where they live. As students work in their groups, circulate to make sure that they are comfortable using map scale to determine approximate distance and that they are using the world map scale (not the U.S. map scale) for this task. When everyone is finished, invite a few students to share their answers and strategies.

Choose other cities for students to determine the distance to, until they are clearly comfortable using the scale on both their U.S. and world maps.

Activity

How Far Away?

Sometimes the things we eat, wear, and use come from close by, and sometimes they come from other cities, states, or countries. We're going to read the labels on different products to find out where things come from. Then, we'll use our maps to estimate just how far away those places are.

Put the transparency of Student Sheet 8, How Far Products Travel, on the overhead. Show one of the packages a student has brought in.

How can we find out where this product comes from?

Reading the label aloud, show the class where you find the origin of the product. Write the product's name and the location of the origin on the transparency. Sometimes distribution or packing location is listed on the label instead of the actual place of origin. Students may use whatever location is given, because it still indicates a distance traveled.

How could we find out, using the maps, how far this product traveled to get to us?

Use this example product to demonstrate finding the distance traveled, and write the results in the last column on the transparency.

Hand out Student Sheet 8, How Far Products Travel. Distribute the labeled product containers or put them in a central place where students can borrow and return them as needed while they fill in their own charts. Students continue to work in small groups, but each student records on his or her own sheet. The group may work together to determine approximately how far each product has traveled to reach them.

Some of the products that students have gathered may come from places that are not labeled on their maps. You will need to decide what choices are available to students in this situation. Following are some options:

■ If you have a class atlas, students can use it to find the location (they may need a quick lesson in using the index). They can then locate it approximately on their own maps, using nearby cities as guides.

■ If you have no class atlas, you might start a list on the board or on chart paper, headed "Does anyone know where this is near?" Students may list the name of any location that they can't find on their maps. Anyone who is familiar with that location can go to the list and write down a nearby city that is labeled on their maps. If there are some locations no one can place, students might use the school library atlas to look up names on the list.

■ Groups might determine approximate distances by, for example, finding the distance to the capital of the state or country where the city is said to be, or to the physical "middle" of that state or country.

Sharing What We Discovered

On the board, make a chart similar to the one shown here, with headings in either miles or kilometers, depending on the scale of the map your students used. This example was generated by a class in Cambridge, Massachusetts. Six column headings should offer a reasonable spread; you may want to add others after you see the data your class has found.

Distribute stick-on notes to each small group. Students record the name of each product, the place it comes from, and the distance traveled on a single stick-on note. They post these in the appropriate columns on the class chart.

Less than 100 km	About 250 km	About 500 km	About 1000 km	About 3000 km	More than 3000 km
apples from Stow, MA 30 km	geoboard from NY 200 km	nickel from Philadelphia 500 km	a card from Cleveland 960 km	hot sauce from New Orleans 2656 km	bowl from Zimbabwe 12,500 km
seltzer from Worcester, MA 80 km	tomato paste from CT 200 km	cereal from NJ 500 km	a car from Detroit 1344 km	Jamaican vegetables 3200 km	fish from China 18,000 km
soccer shirt Allston, MA 8 km		pasta from PA 600 km			tissues from Japan 20,500 km
		coffee from NY 400 km			

What does the chart tell us about how far our products have traveled? What's the farthest distance one of our products has traveled? Have most come from less than 500 kilometers away? What's something else the chart tells us about where our products are from?

Students might, for example, make observations about the typical distance that products travel, whether most have come from close by, or the number of products that have come from outside the U.S.

Sometimes two groups of students will each calculate a different distance for the same location. If the class chart includes any such instances, you might ask those who made the different estimates to meet as a group to compare their strategies for calculating distance, and to think about possible reasons their estimates were different.

If any of the places of origin are especially familiar to the students, they may decide to add some of those distances to their class or personal benchmark lists.

Note: At the end of Session 7, save any product containers labeled by weight or liquid volume for use in Investigation 3. Product containers labeled by weight must be full; those labeled by liquid volume need not be.

Sessions 7 and 8 Follow-Up

 **Homework**

How Far Away?   Distribute Student Sheet 9, How Far Away?, and explain the assignment. On shelves at home or at a market, students look for the product that they think traveled the least distance and the one that traveled the farthest to reach them. They may need to use the classroom maps to figure out the actual distances. They add information about these products to their charts.

 **Extensions**

Where Were You Born?   Students might enjoy locating the places they were born on U.S. and world maps and estimating the distance from their birthplace to the place they live now. Students can then pool and analyze the class data, exploring questions like these: What's the most distant place where one of us was born? How many students were born at least 500 miles from here? How many were born at least 3000 miles from here? Who was born closest to the school?

If students in the class are primarily from the local area, they may explore distances to the birthplaces of parents, grandparents, other relatives, neighbors, or adults in the school.

News Travels, Too Students might bring in postmarked envelopes or postcards and newspaper articles with different datelines to add to the class chart showing distance traveled.

Manufacturing Centers As a connection with social studies, students might use the class data from Student Sheet 8 to investigate additional questions about product origins. For example, do most of our products come from a particular region of the U.S.? Are all the major industrial regions in the U.S. represented in the class data? Do particular kinds of products seem to come from particular regions—for example, are breakfast cereals from a certain region?

Students could investigate these questions by sorting their stick-on notes in different ways, or by using a computer database program that you have access to.

The Global Economy Related social studies investigation: Use the investigation of product origins as a basis for discussing the concept of a global economy. Why do countries import and export? Do the states that package the products actually produce the ingredients as well? If not, where do manufacturers get them? How many states, countries, or continents are involved? Which countries or continents are not represented? If this information is not given on the packaging, students might try writing to companies to learn more. Some companies also provide toll-free numbers for their customers.

Measures of Weight and Liquid Volume

What Happens

Sessions 1 and 2: Grocery Package Contents
Students record measurements they find on the labels of grocery items. They use this information to compare the relative sizes of U.S. standard and metric units of weight and liquid volume. Next, the students each choose an item and line up along a wall of the classroom, in order, according to the weight of their items. They arrange items measured by liquid quantity in a similar manner.

Session 3: Working with Units of Weight
Using materials like foam bits, nails, and sand, students work with balances and weights to make packages that weigh 1 kilogram, 500 grams, 100 grams, 1 gram, 1 pound, and 1 ounce. They make class displays of packages that weigh the same amount—a 1-kilogram display, a 1-pound display, and so on.

Session 4: Working with Units of Liquid Volume Students use calibrated liquid measures to find other containers that hold 1 liter, 500 milliliters, 1 quart, 1 cup, and 1 fluid ounce. They informally compare U.S. standard and metric units of liquid volume.

Session 5: Comparing Weight and Quantity
Students use their displays of weights to begin thinking about the concept of *density*. They list "large" and "small" pounds—things that weigh a pound but take up varying amounts of space. They compare the weights of identical containers filled variously with water, sand, and oil.

Session 6: Writing About Weight and Liquid Measure As an assessment activity, students write to explain in their own words what they know about weight and liquid measure, and to explain how a large object can weigh less than a smaller one.

Sessions 7 and 8 (Excursion): Ordinary and Amazing Vegetables Students collect, organize, and graph data on the weights of several vegetables. They decide which weights are typical for the vegetables they measured. They compare their typical values to a list of vegetable record-breakers, and they create personal benchmarks to relate the record-breaker weights to more familiar objects.

Mathematical Emphasis

- Ordering items by measures of weight and by measures of liquid quantity

- Comparing the relative sizes of U.S. standard and metric measures of weight and liquid quantity

- Developing a sense of the weight of 1 kilogram, 500 grams, 100 grams, 1 gram, 1 pound, and 1 ounce, and developing benchmarks for these measures

- Measuring weight with a balance scale and weights (both metric and U.S. standard)

- Developing a sense of the size of 1 liter, 500 milliliters, 1 milliliter, 1 quart, 1 cup, and 1 fluid ounce, and developing benchmarks for these measures

- Measuring liquid quantity with a liter measure marked in milliliters

- Developing a sense of volume as the amount of space something takes up, or the amount a container can hold

- Distinguishing between quantity and weight

- Beginning to develop meaning for the concept of density

- Using graphs to organize data and to determine typical data

- Developing benchmarks for large weights

What to Plan Ahead of Time

Materials

- Overhead projector (Sessions 1–2, 7–8, Excursion)

- Cans, packages, or bottles labeled by weight and by liquid quantity: 1–2 per pair (Sessions 1–2)

- Balances or scales that measure up to 1.5 kilograms: 3 or 4 (Sessions 3, 5)

- Weights (1 kg, 500 g, 100 g, 1 g, 1 lb, and 1 oz): 2–4 of each per class (Session 3)

- Paper or plastic bags: 10–12 small and 16–18 large bags per class (Session 3)

- Materials that vary in density (Session 3)

- Stick-on notes or masking tape (Sessions 3, 7–8, Excursion)

- Water or sand, and trays to catch spills (Session 4)

- Liquid measuring tools: 1-liter measure (marked in ml), 1-quart and 1-cup measures, 1-fluid-ounce measure (optional): 4 each per class (Session 4)

- Containers that will hold water or sand—some as small as a shot glass (1 oz) and others large enough to hold a liter: 15–20 of various sizes (Session 4)

- Three identical transparent containers; water, vegetable oil, and sand to equally fill them (Session 5)

- Chart paper (Sessions 1–3, 7–8, Excursion)

- Calculators

Other Preparation

- Before Session 5, fill the three identical containers—one with sand, one with water, and one with vegetable oil.

- Duplicate student sheets and teaching resources (located at the end of this unit) in the following quantities. If you have Student Activity Booklets, copy only the items marked with an asterisk.

For Ten-Minute Math

Guess My Unit cards* (pp. 125–126): 1 set per small group. Duplicate (on card stock if possible), cut apart, and clip together sets.

For Sessions 1–2

Student Sheet 10, How Much Does It Weigh? (p. 110): 1 per student, and 1 transparency*

Student Sheet 11, How Much Liquid Inside? (p. 111): 1 per student, and 1 transparency*

Student Sheet 12, Vegetable Weights (p. 112): 1 per student (homework), plus extras* to be used throughout the unit.

For Sessions 3–5

Student Sheet 13, Comparing Weights (p. 113): 1 per student

Student Sheet 14, Things I Know About a Kilogram (p. 114): 1 per student (homework)

Student Sheet 15, Comparing Liquid Quantities (p. 115): 1 per student

Student Sheet 16, Things I Know About a Liter (p. 116): 1 per student (homework)

Student Sheet 17, Feathers or Bricks? (p. 117): 1 per student (homework)

For Sessions 7–8 (Excursion)

Student Sheet 18, Record-Breaker Vegetables (p. 118): 1 per student, and 1 transparency* (optional)

Student Sheet 19, Making Record-Breaker Benchmarks (p. 119): 1 per student (homework)

Grocery Package Contents

What Happens

Students record measurements they find on the labels of grocery items. They use this information to compare the relative sizes of U.S. standard and metric units of weight and liquid volume. Next, the students each choose an item and line up along a wall of the classroom, in order, according to the weight of their items. They arrange items measured by liquid quantity in a similar manner. Students' work focuses on:

- comparing the relative sizes of U.S. standard and metric measures of weight and liquids
- ordering items by measures of weight and by measures of liquid quantity

Materials

- Cans, packages, and bottles labeled by weight and by liquid quantity (1–2 per pair)
- Student Sheet 10 (1 per student, and 1 transparency)
- Student Sheet 11 (1 per student, and 1 transparency)
- Student Sheet 12 (1 per student, homework)
- Overhead projector
- Chart paper (optional)

crackers   170 g. or 6 oz.
tomato sauce   15 oz.
detergent   2 qt (64 fl. oz.)
vanilla   1 fluid oz.
rice   1 lb. 4 g.
pork and beans

Measurements on Grocery Labels

By this point you should have collected ten to twenty grocery items in labeled containers, brought in by you or your students. Distribute these containers so every student or every pair has one to look at.

Let's list the different ways that your containers tell how much food or liquid is inside.

Make a list on the board of some items and the measurements given for those items. Students may need to help one another find the *net contents* of the containers, rather than the amounts of specific ingredients in a single serving.

What do you notice about these measurements? What do they tell us?

Students may notice that liquid and solid quantities are measured differently. As marked on the containers, solids are measured by *weight*. Liquids are not weighed, but are measured by the amount of space they take up. The units used to describe the amount of space they take up are units of liquid capacity. These are a type of volume unit—liquid volume. See the **Teacher Note**, Volume, Capacity, and the Measure of Liquids (p. 52), for discussion of the differences in these volume measures.

How can we tell which grocery items are measured by weight?
How can we tell which ones are measured by liquid capacity?

If there is confusion over the units *ounces* and *fluid ounces,* remind students that although they sound similar, they are different types of measure—*ounces* for weight, and *fluid ounces* for liquid quantities.

Some of the abbreviations that students find on the packaging may be unfamiliar.

Do any of you know what this abbreviation *[write "lb" on the board]* **means? Who knows what this one** *[write "g" on the board]* **means?**

Also check for familiarity with *kg, oz, l, ml, qt, pt,* and *fl oz.* Begin a class list of units of weight and liquid capacity; write both the units and their abbreviations, and keep posted for reference.

A Closer Look at Measures of Weight

We have seen that solid products are measured by weight, but liquids are usually measured by the amount of space they fill up in a container. Let's look more carefully at the products measured by weight, to try to get a sense of how the metric units *grams* and *kilograms* compare with the standard units *ounces* and *pounds*.

Each student or pair needs a package that is labeled by weight. For now, set aside the containers that are labeled with liquid quantities.

On the overhead, show the transparency for Student Sheet 10, How Much Does It Weigh? (or draw a similar chart on the board). Demonstrate how to record weight information from one of the grocery containers.

I'm going to record some information on this chart. The label on this can says that these beans weigh 1 pound. Which column should I write that in? It also says that they weigh 454 grams. Which column should I use for that? So where on the chart should I put the word *beans*? the 454 grams? the 1 pound?

Record the information in the appropriate places.

Name _____   Date _____

How Much Does It Weigh?

Product	Weight of Contents	
	Metric measure 1 kilogram (kg) = 1000 grams (g)	U.S. standard measure 1 pound (lb) = 16 ounces (oz)
dried soup	28 g	1 oz
can of green beans	454 g	1 lb
shredded wheat	283 g	10 oz
ground cinnamon	99 g	3.5 oz

Gather information from students about weights from one or two of their packages and add them to your chart. Encourage students to identify the measures as metric or U.S. standard.

Distribute Student Sheet 10, How Much Does It Weigh? Explain that students will work in pairs, sharing grocery items with the rest of the class, to complete a chart of weights like the one you began on the overhead.

❖ **Tip for the Linguistically Diverse Classroom**   Pair strong English speakers and students with limited English proficiency. They should include small drawings under the *Product* heading on Student Sheet 10 to help identify the packages they have chosen.

Each pair starts with one package that shows its contents measured by weight. Designate a place for students to put these packages when they have finished and to get new ones. Include any extra containers you may have that are labeled by weight.

Students record whatever measures are on the label—metric, U.S. standard, or both. As students work, circulate to ask how they might compare the units of measure—as they are asked to explain in writing under the chart on Student Sheet 10. You might collect and write on chart paper some of the arguments they make. For example:

A pound is 454 grams, and that's smaller than half a kilogram.
A gram is tiny. You need 28 to make an ounce.

Some students may reverse the relationships among units. For example, someone might suggest that 28 grams equal an ounce, so grams are bigger because there are more of them. To clear up such confusion, have a balance scale available so that these students can balance several small objects against one larger one. Ask them to write a sentence to show the relationship, such as "9 erasers balance 1 small pad of paper." Ask, "Which is heavier, 1 eraser or 1 pad of paper?"

Point out that students are to leave the last two rows of the chart on Student Sheet 10 open for the homework assignment.

Activity

A Closer Look at Liquid Measures

When students have written information about five or six products in their Weight of Contents chart, set aside the containers measured by weight (but keep them to be used in the next activity). Introduce Student Sheet 11 on the overhead as you did Student Sheet 10. Set out the containers with liquid quantities where student pairs can take one at a time. Hand out Student Sheet 11, How Much Liquid Inside? Students proceed as they did for Student Sheet 10, filling the chart with information from the packages whose contents are measured by capacity, and leaving room for the homework.

❖ **Tip for the Linguistically Diverse Classroom**   Again, students include small drawings under the *Product* heading to help identify the packages they have chosen.

As you did when students were working with weight measures, circulate and ask how they might compare units of liquid measure in the two systems, metric and U.S. standard.

The chart on Student Sheet 11 will be useful when students work further with liquid quantities in Session 4. After they complete the homework section, suggest that they keep the sheet in a folder or binder for easy reference.

Name _____   Date _____

How Much Liquid Inside?

Quantity of Liquid Contents		
Product	Metric measure 1 liter (l) = 1000 milliliter (ml) 1 milliliter = 1 cubic centimeter (cc)	U.S. standard measure 1 cup = 8 fl oz 1 pint (pt) = 16 fl oz 1 quart (qt) = 32 fl oz 4 quarts = 1 gallon (gal)
salad dressing	474 ml	16 fl oz
detergent	—	64 fl oz 2 quarts
soy sauce	3.8 liter	1 gallon

Activity

Ordering Our Products

This activity will further help students develop a sense of relative amounts as expressed in the two measurement systems.

Ordering by Weight   Each pair of students (or each student, if the class is small or you have enough containers) chooses one of the products labeled by weight to use in this activity. Holding their products, the students line up across the front of the room, in order, according to the weight of their products. That is, the student holding the lightest product is at one end, and the student holding the heaviest product is at the other. Students with items of equal weight take the same place in line, standing one in front of the other. See the **Dialogue Box**, Ordering Our Products by Metric Weights (p. 53), for some issues that arose in one class doing this activity.

When everyone is lined up, the students call out the weights of their products in order, starting with one that weighs the least. If an item is out of place, students reorganize themselves and then continue calling out the weights.

When all the weights have been called out, the students set their products in a line on the floor and take a few minutes to look at the ordered display. Encourage students to discuss any surprises about the size of items in the display.

Do all products with the same weight *look* like they are the same size? Are any small items placed toward the heavy end of the display? Are any large items placed toward the light end of the display? Why? What could be happening? Is the packaging misleading?

Ordering by Liquid Quantity   Repeat the entire activity with items labeled with liquid quantity, if the class collection of products has sufficient variety (with at least six or seven different liquid quantities represented). It's fine to include several containers with the same amount of liquid, as long as they have a different shape.

If you are working in pairs, the students who didn't line up with weights should now line up according to the liquid quantities of their products.

Sessions 1 and 2 Follow-Up

 **Homework**

How Much . . .   Send home the partially completed Student Sheets 10, How Much Does It Weigh?, and 11, How Much Liquid Inside? Point out the homework section on each sheet. Students search their kitchen shelves at home for labeled packages that look *small* but have a *large* weight, and for other products that appear *large* but have a *small* weight. They also look for products that have a very large and a very small liquid volume.

Vegetable Weights   If you are planning to do the excursion in Sessions 7 and 8, Ordinary and Amazing Vegetables, hand out Student Sheet 12, Vegetable Weights, at the end of Session 1. Explain that students should ask an adult for help in taking a trip to the market to weigh "typical" vegetables. From time to time during the next few days, remind students of this assignment, and ask if they have been able to make arrangements to do it.

❖   **Tip for the Linguistically Diverse Classroom**   Bring in several of one of the vegetables listed on Student Sheet 12 (such as potatoes). Include one that is large or small compared to the others. Using these samples, model what the students are assigned to do. Pretend to be at the grocery store. Make clear why you are not selecting the atypical vegetable as you enact choosing one, weighing it, and recording its weight.

Volume, Capacity, and the Measure of Liquids

Volume and *capacity*, and how they relate to *liquid measure*, are easily confused concepts.

The *volume* of a solid object is the amount of space that it occupies, or, if it is hollow, the amount of space enclosed by its outer boundary. Typical units for measuring the volume of solid objects are cubic centimeters and cubic meters (metric), or cubic inches and cubic feet (U.S. standard).

The *capacity* of a container is the amount of space it has into which we can pour a liquid or dry, pourable material. Typical units for measuring capacity are liters and milliliters (metric), or gallons, quarts, pints, cups, and fluid ounces (U.S. standard).

Because we usually measure liquids by pouring them into a container, we generally measure the amount of space that a liquid takes up (its volume) with units of capacity.

So, we say that the *volume* of a room is 30 cubic meters (thinking of it as a hollow, but solid object), while we say that the *capacity* of a soda container is 2 liters. If there is only 1 liter of soda left in the 2-liter container, then we say the contents, or liquid quantity, is 1 liter.

Because these concepts are so closely interrelated, students often confuse them. For example, one student said, "Volume is how much is inside. If there was a big cup and a small cup but they both had the same amount of liquid in them, they would have the same volume." Really, the cups themselves would have neither the same volume nor capacity, but the volume of liquid *held* by the cups would in this instance be the same.

When we speak of volume in this unit, we are referring to the volume of liquids as measured by units of capacity. We deal with solid volume (as measured by cubic units) in the *Investigations* grade 5 unit, *Containers and Cubes* (3-D Geometry: Volume).

DIALOGUE BOX

Ordering Our Products by Metric Weights

As these students are lining up in order by the weight of the contents of their packages (p. 50), they reason about where along the wall they should stand. Their teacher has posted signs along the wall to mark positions for 0 grams, 500 grams, and 1000 grams. Students found themselves clustered near the 500-gram sign.

Katrina: I know I'm going to go close to the 500 sign that Ms. Lopez put up, because I have one that's 454 grams, and that's pretty close to 500.

Leon: So do I! Mine's 454 too.

Becky: And I have one that says 453, so I'll go right before the two of you.

Duc: Mine only says 1 pound. How am I supposed to find my spot?

Mei-Ling: Mine says a pound *and* 454 grams, so they must be the same.

Duc: So I go here too. There's a lot of us.

Kevin: Well, it makes sense that there's a lot of us around there. We found a lot of cans that were about a pound, and a pound is 454 grams.

Becky: Wait. Mine says a pound too, and it says 453 grams. How can that be?

Amy Lynn: It's close. Maybe it's not exactly a pound, and they just rounded it up.

Desiree: Mine only has ounces on it. How do I figure out how many grams are in 10 ounces?

Duc: One ounce is about 28 grams, that should help.

Desiree: If one ounce is 28 grams, then 10 ounces would have to be 280 grams because it's like timesing by 10, you just add a zero.

Greg: Your cereal box can't be only 280 grams. It's enormous! My bag is 300 grams, and it's much smaller.

Desiree: I know this box looks big, but it's 10 ounces, and that means it's not even 300 grams.

Working with Units of Weight

Materials

- Chart paper
- Completed Student Sheet 1 (from Investigation 1)
- Balances or scales that measure up to 1.5 kilograms (3 or 4)
- Metric and standard weights: 1 kg, 500 g, 100 g, 1 g; 1 lb, 1 oz (2–4 of each per class)
- Student Sheet 13 (1 per student)
- Materials that vary in density
- Paper or plastic bags (16–18 large; 10–12 small per class)
- Stick-on notes or masking tape
- Student Sheet 14 (1 per student, homework)

What Happens

Using materials like foam bits, nails, and sand, students work with balances and weights to make packages that weigh 1 kilogram, 500 grams, 100 grams, 1 gram, 1 pound, and 1 ounce. They make class displays of packages that weigh the same amount—a 1-kilogram display, a 1-pound display, and so on. **Note:** If materials are in short supply, half the class can investigate units of weight (Session 3) while the other half investigates units of liquid volume (Session 4). Student work in Session 3 focuses on:

- developing a sense of the weight of 1 kilogram, 500 grams, 100 grams, 1 gram, 1 pound, and 1 ounce, and developing benchmarks for these measures
- measuring weight with a balance scale and weights (both metric and U.S. standard)
- comparing metric and U.S. standard measures of weight by direct measurement

Activity

Discussion: Units of Weight

Measures of Weight	
Units	Benchmarks

Make a two-column chart headed *Measures of Weight*. Label one column *Units* and the other *Benchmarks*. Spend about five minutes on this brief introductory discussion.

What can you tell me about weight? What do we measure when we measure weight? What are some measures of weight you found on the containers? What other units of weight can you think of?

Record student ideas on the chart.

Do you have benchmarks for any of these units? Which of the units on this list can you imagine? Which can you estimate the size of?

Record any appropriate benchmarks that students suggest. Students might refer back to their work in Investigation 1 (as recorded on Student Sheet 1, Exploring Measurement). Suggest that students continue to look for benchmarks they could use for measures of weight throughout the investigation. Post the chart in a convenient place, possibly near your Measures of Length chart from Investigation 1, so that students may refer and add to it throughout this investigation.

In this activity, students will be bagging various materials—wood chips, sand, paper scraps, and the like—to make different weights. The goal is to get from the class as a whole three or four (or more) homemade ("bagged") weights for each of the following: 1 kilogram, 500 grams, 100 grams, 1 gram, 1 pound, and 1 ounce.

Making and Comparing Weights

Lesson Planning Options   You will need to plan how to set up the available materials. One approach is to split the class into four or more groups; each group is then responsible for making one complete set of the six weights. The groups figure out how to share the work so that everyone participates in making at least one weight. Each group will need access to a scale and the appropriate metric and U.S. standard weights.

If measuring tools are limited, another approach is to have half the class do these weight activities (Session 3) while the other half does the liquid volume activities (described in Session 4), then switch for the next session.

Making the Bagged Weights   Form the groups and distribute Student Sheet 13, Comparing Weights, so each student has a copy. Distribute the balances or scales among the groups, but keep the metric and U.S. standard weights in a central place. Students may borrow one weight at a time (or one combination, such as two 50-gram weights to make 100 grams). Show students where they can get bags and where the bins or boxes of different materials are located. Demonstrate briefly how they might make bagged weights. Students might also use classroom objects that they will not be needing in the next couple of days—books, rulers, and the like.

❖ **Tip for the Linguistically Diverse Classroom**   Pair second-language learners with English-proficient students, who should read the instructions and questions on Student Sheet 13 aloud to their partner.

Encourage students to try a variety of materials, so that the final class display will include "big" pounds and "little" pounds, "big" ounces and "little" ounces. For their pound and kilogram weights, some students might use the objects they found in Investigation 1 as benchmarks (recorded on Student Sheet 1, Exploring Measurement).

Things that weigh about 1 kilogram

Things that weigh about 500 g

Things that weigh about 100 g

Things that Weigh about 1 ounce

Things that weigh about 1 pound

Things that weigh about 1 gram

Make labels for the six weights and post them on tables or windowsills where students can display their newly made weights.

Be sure these displays can be left in place through Session 5, when the class will be discussing them further.

As each weight is completed, students label it with the weight and their names (written on a stick-on note or piece of tape) and place it in the appropriate display. To ensure the use of a variety of materials for each weight, suggest that students look at the display of weights already made before they begin each new one. That way they can choose a material that hasn't yet been used for that weight.

Students record a description of each weight their group makes on Student Sheet 13, Comparing Weights. They may use the weights in the class display to find the answers to Part 2, about comparative sizes of U.S. standard and metric units of weight. Since their homemade weights are approximate and the balances may be imprecise, some students might find that 500 grams is more than a pound, some might find that it is less than a pound, and some might find that the two weights are about the same. They can look back at their Weight of Contents chart (Student Sheet 10) to see which is correct.

Looking at the Class Displays When the work is complete and students have cleaned up their materials, they may take a few minutes to look at the objects in each display. Encourage students to pick up the objects to compare them.

Do all the 1-pound weights look and feel as if they weigh about the same thing? What about the 100-gram weights?

When students return to their seats, ask them to share anything they noticed about the weights. For example, students might notice that the size of the weights in a given display varies considerably, or they might notice that a particular book is used for a pound weight, and two of the same book is used as a kilogram weight.

If any of the weights that students made seem like good benchmarks, they may want to add descriptions of them to the class list of weight benchmarks.

Remember to leave the class-made weights on display through Session 5, for a discussion of "big" and "little" pounds.

Session 3 Follow-Up

Things I Know About a Kilogram   Send home Student Sheet 14, Things I Know About a Kilogram, on which students record at least 5 things they know about a kilogram. They might include benchmarks for a kilogram that they found in class; a description of how a kilogram compares to a pound; the number of grams or other units of weight in a kilogram; a description of products they find at home that weigh about a kilogram (or half a kilogram); and how many 250-gram, 500-gram, and 100-gram weights make up a kilogram.

Some teachers like to begin this work in class and use it as a checkpoint for student understanding of measures of weight.

❖ **Tip for the Linguistically Diverse Classroom**   Encourage students with limited English proficiency to share what they have learned about a kilogram by using drawings and mathematical sentences with <, >, and = signs. For example:

 < 1 kilogram
4×250 grams = 1 kilogram

How Much Do You Carry Home?   Students in some classes have enjoyed estimating the weight of the loaded backpack or piles of books they carry home at the end of the school day. Is it more than 1 pound? more than 1 kilogram? more than 2 kilograms? To test their estimates, students get out all the things they will be taking home that day. Have large plastic bags available for students who do not have book bags. Students can check their estimates by weighing their things with a scale or balance.

If you have access to a bathroom scale or a package scale, students can weigh their full bags. If you have only a small balance, students may need to weigh *parts* of the load separately and compute the total. Some students may want to make a large balance (like a seesaw) to test their filled book bags against several weights at once.

Working with Units of Liquid Volume

Materials

- Liter measure marked in milliliters (4 per class)
- Quart and cup measures (4 per class)
- 1-fluid-ounce measure (4 per class, optional)
- Unmarked liquid containers (15–20 of various sizes)
- Student Sheet 15 (1 per student)
- Water or sand
- Trays to catch spills (1 per small group)
- Student Sheet 16 (1 per student, homework)

What Happens

Students use calibrated liquid measures to find other containers that hold 1 liter, 500 milliliters, 1 quart, 1 cup, and 1 fluid ounce. They informally compare U.S. standard and metric units of liquid volume. Student work focuses on:

- developing a sense of the size of 1 liter, 500 milliliters, 1 milliliter, 1 quart, 1 cup, and 1 fluid ounce, and developing benchmarks for these measures
- measuring with a liter measure marked in milliliters
- comparing metric and U.S. standard measures of liquid quantity by direct measurement
- developing a sense of volume as the amount of space something takes up or the amount a container can hold

 Ten-Minute Math: Guess My Unit This is a variation of the Ten-Minute Math activity Guess My Number (pp. 95–96). You will need the Guess My Unit cards (pp. 125–126), one set per small group. You may want to omit the cards with measures of time until Investigation 3.

❖ **Tip for the Linguistically Diverse Classroom** Encourage students to add a small drawing to each card as a visual reminder of the measurement unit—perhaps benchmarks found in class.

Players spread all the cards out in front of them, faceup. The leader secretly picks one of the units, writing the choice on a slip of paper to show later. Players then try to guess the unit selected, taking turns asking yes-or-no questions. For example: Is it metric? Is it a measure of liquid volume? Is it heavier than a pound? Do people use this unit when they cook?

As units are eliminated, players turn those cards facedown. They continue to ask questions until they feel sure of the answer. To discourage random guessing, a player who guesses a unit must explain what clues led to that guess. This discussion should help students begin to think about what makes a good question.

Students can play in groups of three or four. Each group uses one set of unit cards. They rotate the role of leader.

Try to play Guess My Unit once or twice over the next few days, and continue playing it through Investigation 3.

Measuring Capacity

Before You Begin Set up measuring centers with water or sand and trays to catch spillage. At each station, have a 1-liter measure marked in milliliters, a 1-quart measure, and a 1-cup measure. A 1-fluid-ounce measure is optional. Set up your collection of everyday, unmarked containers in a central place; students can borrow and return them as they investigate capacity.

It works best if no more than six students share the same water source or bin of sand. You might set up these centers outside, or in several locations around your classroom.

Using Liquid Measures Distribute Student Sheet 15, Comparing Liquid Quantities, to each student. Direct attention to Part 1. Each group uses the liquid measures with water or sand to find unmarked containers that hold about the five amounts specified in Part 1. Students describe their findings on the student sheet. If there is no container that holds close to a particular quantity, they could mark the level that quantity reaches in a larger container and sketch their findings. They will be completing Part 2 of the sheet in the next activity.

❖ **Tip for the Linguistically Diverse Classroom** Pair second-language learners with English-proficient students, who can help by reading aloud the instructions and questions on Student Sheet 15.

Comparing Liquid Quantities

Students continue to work at the measuring centers in order to answer the questions in Part 2 of Student Sheet 15, Comparing Liquid Quantities. If students have access to a 1-fluid-ounce measure, ask them to add the following question to the sheet: Which is more, 1 fluid ounce or 1 milliliter?

Observing the Students In answering these questions, students compare the size of U.S. standard and metric units, and they find relationships among units of liquid measure in the metric system. As they work, circulate to observe the strategies they use for comparing liquid units. Ask them to tell you about what they are noticing.

Students might compare two amounts by filling a container to the quantity specified and then pouring the sand or water from that container into another. For example, they might fill a quart bottle and then pour the contents into a liter measure to see if a quart is more or less than a liter. Another strategy is to measure out both quantities—say, 500 ml and 1 cup—then pour each into two identical containers (say, quart bottles), and then compare the heights of the contents.

Remind students of their work on Student Sheet 11, How Much Liquid Inside? when they used information on product labels to compare liquid quantities. Does their measuring in this activity confirm what they learned from the labels?

Students who finish early can try estimating liquid amounts, as suggested in the extension for Session 4 (p. 61).

Sharing Our Discoveries   After students have completed the activities and cleaned up, bring the class together for a few minutes. Volunteers describe their strategies for making comparisons.

Which did you find holds more, a liter or a quart? How did you find out?

❖   **Tip for the Linguistically Diverse Classroom**   Volunteers can demonstrate their strategies for comparing the two units of measure.

Since a liter is just a bit more than a quart, students may have found that they are about the same. And, if students spilled a little water in the process of pouring from one container to another, they might even have determined that a quart is a little larger. If there is disagreement among groups, ask them what they can figure out about the comparative size of a liter and a quart from their Quantity of Liquid Contents chart on Student Sheet 11.

Students share any surprises they had about the units they worked with. For example:

Does a teacup really hold 1 cup of liquid?

Are there any containers that look as if they hold more than they really do?

Are there any containers that look as if they have less capacity than they really do?

Are there any two containers that appear to have very different capacities, but in fact hold about the same amount?

Things I Know About a Liter   Students take home Student Sheet 16, Things I Know About a Liter, on which they record at least five things they know about a liter. These might include specific benchmarks for a liter that they found in class, how a liter compares to a quart, the number of milliliters or other units of liquid volume in a liter, a description of products they find at home that contain about a liter or half liter, or about how many liters they drink in a day.

❖ **Tip for the Linguistically Diverse Classroom**   Encourage students with limited English proficiency to share what they have learned about a liter by using drawings and mathematical sentences with <, >, and = signs. For example:

1000 ml = 1 l

 = 1 liter

Some teachers begin this activity in class and use it as a checkpoint.

Estimating Liquid Amounts   For this activity, students work at a measuring center with sand or water, with the calibrated measures, and with three unmarked containers—one wide, one tall and narrow, and the third of medium width. Also have available a supply of rubber bands.

 **Extension**

Students try estimating an amount—say, 500 milliliters—by pouring into the wide container what they guess would be the intended quantity. They then pour the contents into one of the calibrated measures to check. Through continual adjustments, the students get close to the intended amount in the wide container, then mark the height of the contents with a rubber band.

They go through the same process using the tall, narrow container, and compare the height of the contents of the two containers. Students can then test their estimation ability by estimating the same quantity in the medium-width container, and see how close they come.

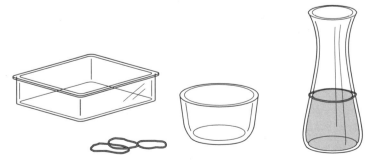

Comparing Weight and Quantity

Materials

- Class displays of weights (from Session 3)
- Three identical transparent containers, all filled to the same level, one with water, one with sand, one with vegetable oil
- Balance or scale (1–2 per class)
- Student Sheet 17 (1 per student, homework)

What Happens

Students use their displays of weights to begin thinking about the concept of *density*. They list "large" and "small" pounds—things that weigh a pound but take up varying amounts of space. They compare the weights of identical containers filled variously with water, sand, and oil. Students' work focuses on:

- distinguishing between quantity and weight
- beginning to develop meaning for the concept of density

Thinking About Density

Draw attention to one of the displays of weights students made in Session 3. Choose *pounds* or any display that includes something large and something small with the same weight.

According to your earlier work, all these things are said to weigh the same—but are they all the same size? Which one of these takes up the most space? Which takes up the least? What material might take up even less space?

Ask students to think of other materials that would make "big" pounds or "little" pounds. List them on the board under the headings *Makes a Big Pound* and *Makes a Little Pound.*

Then, draw attention to a second display that includes both a large and a small weight. Ask the same questions about this display, and record students' responses.

Can anyone guess why things that weigh the same can be different sizes? It has to do with the word *density*. Some of these things are *denser* than others. Dense things are heavy for their size, so you need less to make a certain weight. Here's an old riddle that has been fooling people for years:

What weighs more, a pound of feathers or a pound of bricks?

Ask volunteers to answer the riddle and explain their thinking. Once students have established that both weigh the same, ask them to explain why they think someone might be fooled by the riddle. Just as students have done in creating the displays, the riddle keeps the weight constant but varies the densities.

Show students the three identical containers you prepared, filled to the same level with oil, water, and sand.

I'm going to ask some questions about these three jars. You think about the questions and write your answers on a sheet of paper.

You might note the questions on the board as you ask them.

1. **Is there more water, more oil, or more sand, or the same amount of each? Why do you think so?**
2. **Which do you think weighs more, the water, the oil, or the sand? Or do they weigh the same? Why?**
3. **Is it possible that the same amounts have different weights? Why?**

As students are writing their answers, encourage them to come up and lift the containers. Some students may believe that the water, sand, and oil weigh the same because they are all the same amount. They may need to use a balance scale to see that the substances do not weigh the same. The **Teacher Note**, Learning to Distinguish Between Quantity and Weight (p. 65), further discusses the issues.

Collect students' writing so that you can check their thinking. Then hold a class discussion of the questions.

How could it be that a container of water weighs a different amount than the same size container of sand? How can the container of water and the container of oil weigh different amounts?

Suppose you had 1 liter of ice cream and 1 liter of milk. Do you think they would weigh the same?

What do you think would happen if we poured some sand into the water? Which will be on top, the sand or the water?

What do you think would happen if we poured the oil into the water? Which will be on the top, the oil or water? Why?

For further discussion, you might mention that in official measures of density, water is used as the standard, and we say it has a density of *one*. Things that float are *lighter* than water, or less dense than water; they have a density less than one. Things that sink are more dense than water; they have a density greater than one.

Most wood floats. What does that tell you about the density of wood? Is it greater or less than one?

Look at our lists of "big" and "little" pounds. Which substances do you think would float? Which would sink? Which substances do you think have a density of less than one? Which have a density of more than one?

In earlier activities, students saw that when the weight remains constant, the volume can vary with different densities. In this activity, we are keeping the volume constant, but because the densities vary, the weights are different.

Session 5 Follow-Up

Homework

Feathers or Bricks?   Send Student Sheet 17, Feathers or Bricks?, home with students. Students ask someone outside of school the riddle "Which weighs more, a pound of feathers or a pound of bricks?" Students write down the person's answer and their reasoning. If they want, they can make up variations to this riddle using other substances.

❖ **Tip for the Linguistically Diverse Classroom** Students do this homework in their primary language.

**Extension**

Comparing to the Density of Water Students can explore density further by seeing which substances float and which sink in water. They look for materials that have about the same density as water—those that barely float or that sink very slowly. They might also test their prediction about whether oil is heavier or lighter than water by putting a few drops of oil in a container of water.

Learning to Distinguish Between Quantity and Weight

Many students in the upper elementary grades have difficulty distinguishing between quantity (thought of as the amount of space an item takes up) and weight. Part of this difficulty relates to natural cognitive development: Piaget found that children at a certain level of development may believe that changes of shape will necessarily change weight. For example, some of your students may believe that if you break a lump of clay into smaller pieces it will weigh more than it did as one lump because there are now many pieces—or that it will weigh less because the pieces are smaller. As students continue to interact with and think about the world around them, they will gradually come to see that in such instances, the total weight remains the same.

Students may also have difficulty distinguishing between weight and quantity because they have had little experience with judging these qualities. Even for an adult, estimating the relative amounts in a set of containers can be difficult unless the containers are similar in shape but different in size.

Without scales, weight can also be quite difficult to judge. To compare weights of objects, we need to pick them up, and we can compare only two at a time—one in each hand. If we need to compare weights without touching the objects, we are likely to combine our estimate of quantity with what we know about density. For example, we know that a large container of feathers probably weighs less than a smaller one of water, because feathers are much less dense than water.

Given the chance to experiment with different containers and different materials, students will come to understand differences between weight and quantity. In particular, comparing materials when one of the qualities (weight or quantity) is held constant and the other is varied can help students begin to make distinctions between the two. The activity in Session 3 where weight is held constant (objects of the same weight are grouped together, but their sizes vary), and the activity in Session 5 where quantity is held constant (the three bottles of the same size holding substances of different weights), both provide students with such experiences.

Writing About Weight and Liquid Measure

Materials

- Paper and pencil
- Extra copies of Student Sheet 12 (as needed, homework)

What Happens

As an assessment activity, students write to explain in their own words what they know about weight and liquid measure, and to explain how a large object can weigh less than a smaller one. Students' work focuses on:

- Distinguishing between weight and liquid quantity

Assessment

Describing the Measure of Weight and Liquid Quantity

Ask the students to explain in writing how to measure weight, how to measure liquid quantity, and what those measures mean. For extra credit, they can explain why something can be bigger than another thing but weigh less.

Students can use pictures and examples. They should be clear about the difference between weight and liquid measurement. It works well if they split a page in half, writing "We can measure weight by . . ." and "Weight is . . ." in the top half, and "We can measure liquid quantity by . . ." and "Liquid quantity is . . ." in the bottom half. On the back of the page, they can write about "How one thing can be bigger than another and still weigh less."

Use these papers to assess students' understanding of weight and liquid quantity. Expect all students to have a good sense of the two concepts.

Students will likely describe weight and liquid quantity in different ways. Some students give a general description:

> Weight is how heavy someone or something is. Weight can be pounds, ounces, grams, kilograms, etc.

> When something is very heavy it is very hard to lift. If it is light it is easy to pick up.

> We measure liquids by telling how much is there.

> Liquid quantity is how much space a thing fills up. Example: How much water fills a sink.

Liquid quantity is how much of something there is. There is more quantity in a full liter bottle than a quart bottle because it is a bigger bottle so more can go into a liter.

Other students may show that they know generally how these words are used by giving examples, but may not give a good description.

Weight is like a man or a woman who is fat and really heavy.

Liquid quantity is what you pour out of a jar.

....

❖ **Tip for the Linguistically Diverse Classroom** Conduct this assessment orally for students with limited English proficiency. Ask them to point out actual objects (or draw simple pictures of objects) that we use to measure *weight* and to measure *liquid quantity.* To further check student understanding, ask questions that can be answered yes or no. For example:

Can we measure weight by *pounds?*
Do we measure liquids with a ruler?

....

we can measure weight by putting things on a scale.

weight is how easy or hard it is to pick something up. That is weight.

anvil → Heavy

↓ light

Session 6 Follow-Up

Vegetable Weights If you are planning to do Sessions 7 and 8, Ordinary and Amazing Vegetables, this is the last chance for students to weigh vegetables at the market and bring in their information about the weights. Hand out extra copies of Student Sheet 12, Vegetable Weights, as needed.

 **Homework**

Ordinary and Amazing Vegetables

Materials

- Students' Vegetable Weights (Student Sheet 12, completed homework)
- Stick-on notes (6–8 per student)
- Chart paper
- Student Sheet 18 (1 per student; 1 transparency, optional)
- Student Sheet 19 (1 per student, homework)
- Calculators
- Overhead projector (optional)

What Happens

Students collect, organize, and graph data on the weights of several vegetables. They decide which weights are typical for the vegetables they measured. They compare their typical values to a list of vegetable record-breakers, and they create personal benchmarks to relate the record-breaker weights to more familiar objects. Students' work focuses on:

- using graphs to organize data
- using graphs to determine typical data
- developing benchmarks for large numbers of pounds
- determining relative quantities; how many times as heavy as another or how many times as long as another an object is

Organizing Data About Vegetables

Students begin by copying the information from their homework, Student Sheet 12, Vegetable Weights, onto stick-on notes. They use a different note for each vegetable they weighed. On the note, they specify the name of the vegetable, its weight, and their initials or other identification.

Next, the students form groups that focus on one kind of vegetable. They work together to organize, display, and report their data about, say, cauliflower size. If there are more vegetables than groups, assign the vegetables for which you have the most data and keep the others for groups that want to explore the data for a second vegetable.

Each group begins by collecting all the stick-on notes with data about its vegetable. For example, the cauliflower group will collect stick-on notes from everybody who weighed cauliflower. Using a sheet of large paper and their stick-on notes, they create a sketch graph that represents all the weights recorded for their vegetable.

For more information, see the **Teacher Note**, Sketch Graphs: Quick to Make, Easy to Read (p. 73). Assure students that their sketch graphs need not be beautiful, only accurate and easy to understand. Students may need to graph their data in several different ways before they find an arrangement that they think communicates the data points. They may decide they need to label the categories they create on their graphs, or they may decide that the arrangement of stick-on notes speaks for itself and needs no labels.

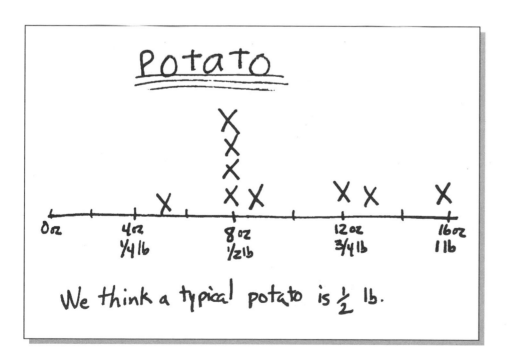

Observing the Students While students are working, walk around the room and ask groups to refine their representations if necessary. For example, some groups may not use equal intervals for displaying data: If they have data on lettuces that weigh 2 pounds, 2¼ pounds, and 2¾ pounds, they may need a reminder to include a 2½ (or 2²/4) pound category as well—even though it will be empty.

Groups may also need help choosing an appropriate *interval* for the range of data they are working with. For example, lettuce weighing from 1 to 3 pounds might be grouped by ¼ pounds, but pumpkins ranging in weight from 3 to 15 pounds might be better grouped by whole pounds. Students would then need to decide how to handle the weights with fractional parts.

Once a group's graph is complete, students use it to decide the *typical* weight of their vegetable.

As you look at your set of data, what might you say is the typical weight of the vegetables we investigated?

Students show their graphs to the class and explain how they decided what was typical. Some students may have arrived at a single typical value, while others will describe a typical range. Compile the typical weights for all the vegetables on a piece of chart paper and post it where everyone can see it; they will be copying the data later in these sessions.

Activity

Revealing the Vegetable Record-Breakers

Before distributing Student Sheet 18, Record-Breaker Vegetables (based on information in National Geographic *World,* October 1991), ask students to predict how heavy the record-breakers are. To heighten the drama, ask for their predictions and reveal the results one vegetable at a time. If you use the transparency of this sheet, uncover one vegetable at a time.

Our typical cabbage was 2 to 3 pounds. Our heaviest cabbage was 5 pounds. What are your predictions about how heavy the record-breaker cabbage is?

Elicit many predictions and jot them down on the chalkboard. Then reveal the record-breaker statistic. Continue in this way for all the vegetables.

Distribute Student Sheet 18, Record-Breaker Vegetables. Students copy into the second column the typical weights listed on their class chart. They then figure out the last column: how many times as heavy the record-breaker vegetable is. Possible strategies students might use include division or multiplication with a calculator, or repeated addition or subtraction. Students should turn any "messy" decimals that appear on the calculator into approximate answers, writing the whole numbers that the decimal numbers are between.

Observing the Students   While students are working, observe their strategies. Does everyone have a way to find how many times as large the record breaker is? Do they have a way of estimating without the calculator? Can they make sense of many-digit decimals on the calculator? After students have worked on one or two vegetables, ask them to pause so they can hear each other's strategies.

How did you figure out how many times as heavy the record-breakers are?

Invite students to come up to the board or to use the overhead to show their methods. After all the different strategies have been described, students finish Student Sheet 18.

To help students make sense of the record-breaker vegetable data, Student Sheet 19 asks them to find personal benchmarks for these weights.

We just found out that the heaviest recorded cauliflower is about 53 pounds. We now need a sense of just how heavy that is. Are there any weights you are familiar with that you can use as benchmarks?

If the students are stumped, encourage them to think about the weight of a pet, a relative, or a friend. Students could also use facts they have learned in social studies or science as comparison points—for example, the weight of a baby Orca whale.

Some students may think of benchmarks that are just about the same weight as the vegetables. For example, one student said, "The record-breaker cauliflower weighs 53 pounds, which is about as heavy as my little sister." Encourage them to find benchmarks that are based on *number of times as heavy as* familiar weights as well.

Abby tells us that her cat weighs 7 pounds. How many of her cats would make up the record-breaking 25-pound lettuce? How many times as heavy is the lettuce?

Students work on finding meaningful benchmarks for at least three of the record-breaker vegetables.

Sessions 7 and 8 Follow-Up

 **Homework**

Making Record-Breaker Benchmarks   Students continue to work on Student Sheet 19, finding benchmarks for the weights of the record-breaker vegetables. Also send home students' completed copies of Student Sheet 18, Record-Breaker Vegetables, for use as a reference.

 **Extensions**

Adding Record-Breakers to the Graphs   Students might figure out how much longer their sketch graphs would need to be in order to accommodate the new record-breaker data. They would have to think about how long their original graphs are and how many more intervals they would need to add to include the record-breaker data. In many instances, as for the 817-pound pumpkin, it is more manageable to figure out the length of paper they would need in order to include the new data, rather than to actually make the new graph. Students might tape a piece of string or adding machine tape to their original graphs to demonstrate this added length.

Which Is the Most/Least Expensive?   Students look for the most or least expensive food items sold in a grocery store. The class decides how they will compare prices: cost per gram? per ounce? They write the name of the product, the size and price information for any that might qualify, and how they figured the price per unit. Post these. Add to the collection as students find more or less expensive items.

Sketch Graphs: Quick to Make, Easy to Read

Graphing is often taught as an art of presentation, the end point of the data analysis process, the means for communicating what has been found. Certainly, a pictorial representation is an effective way to present data to an audience at the end of an investigation. But graphs, tables, diagrams, and charts are also data analysis tools. A user of statistics employs pictures and graphs frequently *during the process of analysis* in order to better understand the data.

Many working graphs need never be shown to anyone else. Students can make and use them just to help uncover the story of the data. We call such representations *sketch graphs* or *rough draft graphs*.

Sketch graphs

- can be made rapidly, without careful measurement or scaling
- reveal aspects of the shape of the data
- are clear, but not necessarily neat
- don't require labels or titles (as long as students are clear about what the graphs represent)
- don't require time-consuming attention to color or design

Encourage students to invent different forms of sketch graphs until they discover some that work well in organizing their data. Sketch graphs might be made with pencil and paper, with interlocking cubes, or with stick-on notes. Cubes and stick-on notes offer flexibility because they can easily be rearranged.

A line plot is particularly useful for a first look at numerical data. It clearly shows the range of the data and how the data are distributed over that range. Line plots work especially well for numerical data with a small range.

A simple working line plot need not have a title, labels, or a vertical axis. It can be simply a sketch showing the values of the data along a horizontal axis, with X's stacked up to mark the

frequency of those values in the data set. For example, if 15 students have just collected data on the number of commercial minutes in a half-hour TV show (as they will do in Investigation 3), a line plot showing their data might be sketched as shown below.

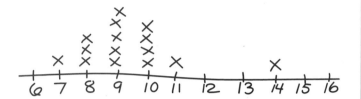

At a glance, we can tell from this plot that although the *range* is from 7 to 14, the *interval* in which most data falls is from 8 to 10. The *outlier,* at 14, appears to be an unusual value, separated by a considerable gap from the rest of the data.

One advantage of a line plot is that we can record each piece of data directly as we collect it. To set up a line plot, students start with an initial guess about what the range of the data is likely to be: What should we put as the lowest number? How high should we go? Leave some room on each end of the line plot so that you can lengthen the line later if the range includes lower or higher values than you expected.

Data with a wide range will need to be clumped. For example, to show the range in age of the oldest person in the students' households, the line plot might span five-year intervals, perhaps with a range from 25–29 to 100–104.

By quickly sketching data in line plots on the chalkboard, you provide a model of using such graphs to get a quick, clear picture of the shape of the data.

It's About Time

What Happens

Session 1: Estimating Half a Minute Students make a list of units for measuring time and begin to chart benchmarks they already use for any of these units. Then they estimate the passage of 30 seconds and graph how their estimates change with increased practice.

Session 2: Commercial Minutes Students analyze data collected at home on the number of commercial minutes in a half-hour television show. They use their data and national statistics to estimate how much time an average fifth grader spends watching commercials each year.

Session 3: Making Sense of Years Students compare people's ages in two ways: "how many years older" and "how many times as old." They make strips out of one-centimeter graph paper to represent the years of their lives to date, and the lives of adults whose ages they have learned. They use these strips in making age comparisons.

Mathematical Emphasis

■ Developing vocabulary for units of time

■ Developing benchmarks for minutes and for years

■ Timing in minutes and seconds

■ Collecting, displaying, and analyzing data

■ Using measurement conversions (minutes to hours to days) in the problem-solving process

■ Keeping track of computations in a multistep problem

What to Plan Ahead of Time

Materials

- Clock or watch with a second hand: 1 per small group, or use the classroom clock (Session 1)
- Calculators (Sessions 2–3)
- Overhead projector (Session 2, optional)
- Scissors (Session 3)
- Tape (Session 3)
- Chart paper (Sessions 1–3)
- Construction paper (Session 3, optional)

Other Preparation

- Duplicate student sheets and teaching resources (located at the end of this unit) in the following quantities. If you have Student Activity Booklets, no copying is needed.

For Session 1

Student Sheet 20, Estimating 30 Seconds (p. 120): 1 per student

Student Sheet 21, Commercial Minutes (p. 121): 1 per student (homework)

For Session 2

Student Sheet 22, Adults' Ages (p. 122): 1 per student (homework)

For Session 3

Student Sheet 23, Comparing Ages (p. 123): 1 per student

One-centimeter graph paper (p. 124): 2–3 sheets per student

- Review the process of making a line plot. Refer to the **Teacher Note**, Sketch Graphs: Quick to Make, Easy to Read, p. 73. (Session 2)

- Cut strips of centimeter paper (1 cm = 1 year), making demonstration "lifetime" strips to represent the ages of an adult and a child in your life. Pick a child younger than your students. (Session 3)

Estimating Half a Minute

What Happens

Students make a list of units for measuring time and begin to chart benchmarks they already use for any of these units. Then they estimate the passage of 30 seconds and graph how their estimates change with increased practice. Their work focuses on:

- developing benchmarks for units of time
- using an analog clock to time in seconds
- estimating 30 seconds
- graphing repeated trials

 Ten-Minute Math: Guess My Unit Once or twice during this investigation, outside of math class, continue to play Guess My Unit, the variation of Guess My Number that was introduced as Ten-Minute Math for Investigation 2 (see p. 58). As needed, restore the cards for units of time for use during this investigation.

Materials

- Chart paper
- Clock or watch with a second hand (1 per group)
- Student Sheet 20 (1 per student)
- Student Sheet 21 (1 per student, homework)

Activity

Discussion: Units of Time

Measures of Time	
Units	Benchmarks

In preparation for this brief introductory discussion, make a two-column chart titled *Measures of Time*. Label one column *Units* and the other *Benchmarks*. Post the paper in a convenient place, possibly with your other "Measures" charts, so that students may refer and add to it throughout this investigation.

So far in this unit we've measured length and distance—how long or how far away something is. We've measured weight—how heavy things are— and we've measured liquid quantities. Now we're going to talk about *time.* **Is time something we can measure? How? What are some units we use to measure time?**

Record students' suggestions on the chart. Common time measures such as *second, minute, hour, day, week, month,* and *year* will probably be on your list. There are less common measures that might intrigue some students, including *fortnight, decade, century,* and *millennium.* Introduce some of these by using them in a familiar context (for example, "We live in the twentieth century.") and discuss what they mean.

Note: If anyone suggests *light year* as a unit of time, briefly explain that the light year is a commonly misunderstood unit. A light year is a measure of distance, *not* a measure of time; it is the distance light travels in a year, approximately 5.878 trillion miles. If the term comes up, students can add it to their chart that lists units of length and distance.

Do you have benchmarks for any of these units?

Record on the chart any appropriate benchmarks that students suggest. You might remind them of the work they did at the beginning of this unit (on Student Sheet 1, Exploring Measurement), when they found things that would take about 1 minute.

Reading the Second Hand

Many students are familiar with digital watches. Ask students not to use their digital watches during this part of the activity, but to use the position of the second hand on an analog clock to compute elapsed time. This will give them exposure to and practice in reading a clock with a dial face.

Have you ever heard people say, "Just a second"? Usually they mean more than 1 second, because a second is a very short period of time. Today we're going to be timing a period of 30 seconds. Before we begin, let's practice using the clock to tell how many seconds have passed.

Tell the class you will say "Start" and then "Stop," and they are to decide how many seconds went by in between. If everyone is looking at the same classroom clock, start timing when the second hand is exactly on the twelve. Do this two or three times, stopping after irregular intervals such as 19 seconds or 34 seconds.

If your students are ready for an extra challenge, start timing when the second hand is on a different 5-second interval. Some students may find it easier if they write down starting and ending times in seconds and then compute the elapsed time.

Estimating 30 Seconds

Now you will see how close you can get to estimating 30 seconds without looking at a clock or watch.

Before you send students off to work in groups, model the activity. Make a group of three, with yourself as the timekeeper for two students.

You will work in groups of three and take turns being the timekeeper. The timekeeper can use the clock or a watch. When a new minute starts, the timekeeper says "Start." The rest of you close your eyes and try to estimate 30 seconds. Raise your hands, silently, when you think 30 seconds have gone by.

The timekeeper needs to watch the clock carefully and jot down the actual time as each person responds. The timekeeper shouldn't tell anybody's time until everyone in the group has responded, even if it's after 30 seconds. After you raise your hand, keep your eyes closed. Don't open your eyes until the timekeeper tells you everyone has finished. The timekeeper will tell you what your estimates were. Someone else becomes timekeeper after three trials.

In a practice round, demonstrate how to quickly note each student's estimated time.

After each round, write down your own estimate for that trial. It is important to record your estimates *in the order of the rounds* so that later you will be able to look for patterns in your progress.

Give students time to complete one or two trials. Get around quickly to find out how students are estimating 30 seconds. If you find that some students have good ideas but others don't, stop the class briefly and ask some students to share their methods. If there is enough diversity within groups, suggest that students tell their partners their strategies.

Students might use four-syllable words to gauge passing seconds; for example: one huckleberry, two huckleberry, three huckleberry (you might also hear *Mississippi, alligator,* or *banana split).* Or, they might chant 1 one-two-three, 2 one-two-three, 3 one-two-three, and so forth. Others might picture the second hand moving on the clock, or tap out the rhythm with hands or feet.

Keep estimating. Remember to switch timekeepers after every three trials and to stop after everybody has had a turn to be the timekeeper. At the end, everybody should have made at least six estimates. If you have time, do ten estimates each.

Students who make ten estimates will be able to work more easily with percents if they do the extension activity, Summarizing Data (p. 80).

Graphing the Estimates

As groups complete their 6–10 estimates, hand out Student Sheet 20, Estimating 30 Seconds.

You have just collected lots of data about how long your sense of 30 seconds actually is. Now it is time to organize and present your data. On this sheet, make a graph showing all your estimates in the order you made them. Include only your own estimates, not those of other people in your group. Be sure to show the order in which your estimates happened so that we can see how they changed as you did more trials.

Below the graph, students write about how and why their estimates changed.

❖ **Tip for the Linguistically Diverse Classroom** Students with limited English proficiency may respond orally to tasks 2 and 3. Help them by asking questions that require only a one-word response. For example:

Did your estimates get better with practice?
Did you count something to estimate 30 seconds?
What did you count?

Preparing for Homework Leave a few minutes at the end of class to explain the homework, when students will be timing commercial minutes in a TV program. They will need this data for Session 2. Refer to the Session 1 Follow-Up for details.

Session 1 Follow-Up

Commercial Minutes Hand out Student Sheet 21, Commercial Minutes, to each student.

 **Homework**

How many minutes of a 30-minute television show do you think are taken up with commercials? Take a minute to discuss your estimate with a neighbor.

Tonight we're going to find out how good your estimates are.

Students may watch any half-hour TV show of their choice (with parental permission). As they watch, students will need to have a timing device that shows seconds. If students do not watch television at their house, they have no homework. The data other students collect will be plenty for everyone to work with. The procedure is as follows:

Before the show begins, students record the name of the show, the day of the week, and the time it begins. They should have their timing device, Student Sheet 21, and a pencil ready to go when the show starts.

Students must start and stop timing exactly on the half-hour or hour. The half-hour is likely to begin and end with a commercial. These commercials count because they are *within* the half-hour allotted for the show.

They write down the time whenever the program stops for a commercial, and write down the time when the show starts again. Remembering to do the timing, especially if the viewer is engaged by the show, can be difficult. Students might want to enlist family members to help them keep on task. They need not time each individual commercial, but only the total time of each commercial break.

When the show is over, students figure out the duration of each commercial break and add up all the times to find the total.

❖ **Tip for the Linguistically Diverse Classroom** If possible, model the instructions for this assignment while watching a real TV show with commercials in class. Take the students through each step of the timing and recording process. If no TV is available in the classroom, draw one on the board. Pretend to watch a commercial, and model what students are supposed to do.

Students will need to bring their results to school for Session 2. As students come into class, have them list their data (name of show and total commercial minutes) on the board or on chart paper so that it will be collected before class discussion.

 **Extension**

Summarizing Data Students might try using either fractions or percents to summarize the data shown on their Student Sheet 20, Estimating 30 Seconds. For example, they might look at what percentage of their estimates were above, below, or exactly at 30 seconds; or they might figure what fraction or percentage were within a certain range (say, within 5 seconds of the goal). Students could also pool results and analyze the class data with fractions or percentages.

❖ **Tip for the Linguistically Diverse Classroom** Students may bring in a pictorial list of two-minute chores.

Commercial Minutes

What Happens

Students analyze data collected at home on the number of commercial minutes in a half-hour television show. They use their data and national statistics to estimate how much time an average fifth grader spends watching commercials each year. Their work focuses on:

- solving problems involving a series of related calculations
- using measurement conversions in the problem-solving process
- making and interpreting line plots
- using real-world knowledge to evaluate a statistic

Materials

- Chart paper
- Completed Student Sheet 21 (from Session 1 homework)
- Calculators
- Overhead projector (optional)
- Student Sheet 22 (1 per student, homework)

Activity

Commercials: Analyzing the Data

As students arrived in class, they should have been listing on a prepared class chart the results of their homework (Student Sheet 21). Before you begin this discussion of the collected data, ask if anyone has any more data to add.

At home, you collected these data about the number of commercial minutes that are included in a half-hour television show. Let's organize your data on a line plot.

Students can help you set up the line plot on the overhead or the board, suggesting the range and checking off each piece of data as you or another student record it on the line. (The **Teacher Note**, Sketch Graphs: Quick to Make, Easy to Read, p. 73, offers a review of making line plots.) Ask students to approximate partial minutes to the nearest minute.

As we look at this set of data, what might we say is *typical* about the number of commercial minutes in a half-hour show?

Students may think about this in different ways. Some might think what's typical is the number of minutes that occurs the most often (mode). Others might look for the number in the middle of a clump. Try to come to an agreement on a typical number, or perhaps two. Then look at the range of the data. What might be the reasons for the extremes?

The **Teacher Note**, The Shape of the Data: Clumps, Bumps, and Holes (p. 84) suggests ways to help students find meaning in their line plot. The **Dialogue Box**, Finding the Typical Number of Commercial Minutes (p. 85), excerpts a class discussion of a line plot.

What could be some reasons that different shows have different numbers of commercial minutes?

Differences may be attributed to time of day, type of show, or to whether the intended audience is adults or children. Students may be interested in looking at how the commercials were spaced out within the show.

Why do you think advertisers space commercials out the way they do? Were they spaced out evenly throughout the show?

Activity

Discussion: How Much TV Do We Watch?

Ask students to estimate how many hours a week a typical fifth grader watches TV. Quickly go around the class as you write all estimates on the board. (There is no need to attribute estimates to particular individuals.)

According to the *1995 Information Please Almanac* [Boston: Houghton Mifflin, 1994], American children between the ages of 6 and 11 typically watched 24.5 hours of television a week. Do you think you watch about the typical amount, or do you watch more or less?

Students may need some time to work out about how much TV they watch. For example, they might need to write down the shows they watch each day, and then total the number of hours for the week. If many of your students watch more or fewer than the typical number of hours, explore with them why this might be so.

Activity

Assessment

A Year's Worth of Commercials

We know how much TV a typical fifth grader watches in a week. Think about how we could figure out how many hours of *commercials* you typically watch in an entire year.

Write these questions on the board:

> About how many hours of commercials does a typical fifth grader watch in a year?
>
> How does your TV-watching compare with what's typical?

Before you start figuring, you'll need to decide which number to use for the typical commercial minutes in a half hour.

I want you to answer this question as a written report. Write down all the computations you do as you figure out the problem—even write down those you compute with a calculator.

After you find how many commercial hours a typical fifth grader watches in a year, write a few sentences about how your TV-watching compares. That is, do you think you watch that many hours of commercials in a year? Do you think your classmates do? Why might other American children watch more or fewer hours than you do?

As students begin to work on this problem, some issues may arise. For example, students may argue that American children spend some of their viewing time watching shows on public television, which has virtually no commercials. They also may theorize that hour-long shows have proportionately fewer commercials than half-hour shows. Encourage students to think about these and other factors.

For your assessment of student work, it's important that they write down all their calculations. If they use a calculator, they write down both the numbers they entered in the calculator and the results. They also need to *label* the results of each step—for example, the number of hours watched in a day, or in a week.

Students may ask you for basic facts they need in order to solve the problem, such as 60 minutes = 1 hour, 365 days = 1 year, and 52 weeks = 1 year. Supply this information freely. If the need seems widespread, quickly write on the board a list of facts students might need as they continue to work on the problem.

After they finish the computations, partners trade reports to make sure someone else can follow their steps as written. They add anything needed to clarify their work, then write a few sentences about their answer and how "typical" they think they are.

As students finish and ask you to look at their work, read it through. Ask them to add information about anything that is not clear. In particular, be sure they have labeled numbers along the way so that you can follow all the steps of their computation. See the **Teacher Note**, Assessment: A Year's Worth of Commercials (p. 86), for some notes on what to look for in student work.

Session 2 Follow-Up

Adults' Ages   Distribute Student Sheet 22, Adults' Ages, and describe the homework. For class use in Session 3, students find out the ages of four adults in their lives. At least one of the adults should be a parent or someone of their parents' generation. Another should be a grandparent or someone of their grandparents' generation. Remind students to bring this list of four names and ages for the next math class.

 **Homework**

Extensions

Hours and Hours of Commercials The activity A Year's Worth of Commercials can be extended to a personal level, as students estimate how many hours of television they themselves watch in a week. Using the data on commercial minutes collected by the class, they can also approximate how many hours of commercials they personally watch in a year. Some might be interested in writing a brief statement on how they are affected by all these commercials.

Benchmarks for Other Units of Time Students might like to choose one or more periods of time (such as 15 minutes, 2 hours, or 1 week) and determine personal benchmarks for them. For example, they might decide that a music lesson, a half-hour TV show, or the drive to a relative's house would be their benchmark for 30 minutes.

One issue that might arise for students working on this extension is the subjective nature of time. That is, a half-hour music lesson can pass very quickly one day and be excruciatingly slow another day. The goal for establishing time benchmarks is simply to gradually develop a sense of different periods of time—minutes, hours, days, weeks, months, and years.

Teacher Note

The Shape of the Data: Clumps, Bumps, and Holes

Describing and interpreting data is a skill that must be acquired. Too often, students simply read numbers or other information from a graph or table without any interpretation or understanding. It is easy for students to notice only isolated bits of information (for example, "Vanilla got the most votes," "Five people were 50 inches tall") without developing any overall sense of what the graph shows. Looking at individual numbers in a data set without looking for patterns and trends is something like decoding the individual words in a sentence without comprehending the meaning of the sentence.

To help students pay attention to the shape of the data—its patterns and special features—we have found it useful to use such words as *clumps, clusters, bumps, gaps, holes, spread out,*

bunched together, and so forth. Encourage students to use this casual language about shape to describe where most of the data are, where there are no data, and where there are isolated pieces of data.

A discussion of the shape of the data often begins with identifying the special features of the data: Where are the clumps or clusters, the gaps, the outliers? Are the data spread out, or are lots of the data clustered around a few values? Later on students decide how to interpret the shape of these data: Do we have theories or experience that might account for how the data are distributed?

By focusing on the broad picture, the shape of the data, we discover what those data have to tell us about the world.

Finding the Typical Number of Commercial Minutes

For the discussion of the number of commercial minutes in a half-hour TV show (p. 82), the teacher made a line plot from the data students collected. Small groups analyzed the data to find the typical number of minutes per show, and here they are meeting as a class to share their ideas.

```
              X
    X    X    X
    X    X    X
    X    X    X
    X    X    X    X
    X    X    X    X    X              X
  ──────────────────────────────────────────
    6    7    8    9   10   11   12   13   14
```

Jasmine: We think you should pick the number that happens a lot, so we picked 9, because there are more 9's than any other number.

What do other people think?

Corey: We did that too. There are a lot of 9's, so that seemed like what was typical.

Did anyone choose another number for typical?

Christine: We came up with 10.

So your choice is a little higher than what Jasmine's group and Corey's group picked. How did you come up with that?

Christine: We just picked the middle number.

What do you mean by "the middle number"?

Christine: Because it's in the middle, between 7 and 13.

Oh, so you looked at the range of our data and found the middle number along the bottom of the line plot?

Christine: Yeah.

Natalie: But there are lots more crowded around the 8 and 9 and there are none at 12, so I don't think you should count the higher numbers the same as the lower ones.

So, Natalie, you're looking at the clumps, where the X's actually fall. Does that influence your thinking about what's typical?

Manuel: You could find the middle X, not the middle number.

How would you do that?

Manuel: Like, just cancel out the top and the bottom X and then keep going. Cancel out the second highest and the second lowest X, then the third highest and the third lowest X until you get down to one number.

That is called the median.

Amy Lynn: You don't get just one number. You get two numbers—8 and 9.

Manuel: OK, so call it eight and a half.

Using Manuel's canceling out method, we get down to two numbers, an 8 and a 9. Does anyone have a different way to describe what's typical using his method?

Yu-Wei: We could say it's 8 *or* 9.

Rachel: Or *between* 8 and 9.

Becky: But 7 happens a lot too. I think it is 7, 8, or 9.

I wonder what we would find if we collected more data from different shows.

Encourage all invented methods that make sense. This is not to suggest that *any* method is as good as any other; expect the students to reflect on whether or not their results are reasonable and useful. Juxtaposing one student method with another, as the teacher does in this discussion, is often a good way to help students think about the reasonableness of their method. Many of the students' ideas will help them understand standard measures of center, such as the median and the mode, which they will encounter in the *Investigations* grade 5 unit on data analysis, *Data: Kids, Cats, and Ads.*

Assessment: A Year's Worth of Commercials

In this assessment, students put together almanac data and data they gathered to find about how many hours of commercials a typical fifth grader watches in a year. Answers will vary, depending on the class data used.

The assessment shows you if students can choose workable strategies and if they can keep track of their computations as they solve this multistep problem. As you evaluate their work, consider the following:

- Did the students organize the problem into manageable steps that make sense?

- Did the students record their steps clearly, labeling the numbers so that others can follow what was done?

- Did the students' computation help them approximate a reasonable answer? Were they able to convert minutes to hours?

- Did they include written comments comparing themselves with what's typical?

Katrina (below, left) has done a nice job. She has not labeled every one of the numbers she used in the computation, but it is reasonably easy to follow her steps. Her answer will not be as high as some because she rounded 24.5 to 24 and used 4 weeks/month, 12 months/year (short of the 52 weeks in a year), but her figure is close enough for this type of estimate.

Desiree has done an excellent job of labeling until she gets to the division step, where she divides the number of hours of TV watched in a year by the number of commercial minutes in an hour. Here she did not label her numbers, and perhaps as a result her choice of computation does not make sense.

Both Katrina and Desiree made a thoughtful analysis of how their own TV-watching compares with the typical.

Katrina

24 hours and 30 minutes a week

2 shows — 1 hour — 17 minits comercals

408 minits of comercals

408 in a week

408 × 4 weeks = 1632 minits a month

1632 × 12 = 19,584

326 hours of comercals in a year

60) 19,584

I don't think I watch this many because I can only watch a haf hour of TV a day and that is a lot less.

Desiree

10 min. of commercials
× 2
20 min. in 1 hour

365 days in 1 year
3.5 hours tv a day
1095
182
1277 hours in 1 year of tv

63 17/20 hours of commercials in 1 year
20) 1277
1200
77
60
17

I don't think I watch this much tv because I don't watch very much. I think maybe kids watch a lot more tv in the winter and if they live where its not very safe to play outside.

Making Sense of Years

What Happens

Students compare people's ages in two ways: "how many years older" and "how many times as old." They make strips out of one-centimeter graph paper to represent the years of their lives to date, and the lives of adults whose ages they have learned. They use these strips in making age comparisons. The students' work focuses on:

- determining how many years older, numerically and with a paper strip model
- determining how many times as old, numerically and with a paper strip model
- finding and comparing ways to express a fractional part
- using their age as a benchmark to develop meaning for longer periods of time

Materials

- Chart paper (optional)
- Teacher-prepared "life-time" strips for an adult and a younger child
- One-centimeter graph paper (2–3 sheets per student)
- Scissors
- Tape
- Student Sheet 23 (1 per student)
- Calculators
- Construction paper (optional)

Activity

How Many Times as Old? How Much Older?

On chart paper or on the board, set up a chart like the one below.

How old are you, Mei-Ling? If you are 11 years old, how old would some-one be who is _twice_ as old as you? What about someone who is _three_ _times_ as old as you? _Seven_ times? How do you know?

Record this information on the chart. Gather the same information from students of different ages in your class. Encourage students to share their strategies for determining multiples of their ages. Typically, students will use either repeated addition or multiplication, or a combination of the two.

Someone three times as old as me would be 11 + 11 + 11, or 33.

I am 9, so someone 4 times as old as me would be 9 × 4, or 36.

Name	Age	Age of someone 2 times as old	Age of someone 3 times as old	Age of someone 7 times as old	Age of someone 10 times as old
Mei-Ling	11	22	33	77	110
Leon	9	18	27	63	90
Maricel	10	20	30	70	100

Maricel said that she is 10 years old, and that someone who is twice as old as she would be 20. Now here's a different question: How many *years* older than Maricel is that person?

Some students may recognize the different concepts behind these questions: that one involves multiplication and the other addition or subtraction. Other students may be able to answer both questions correctly, but not be able to verbalize the concepts behind them. Continue to ask different students until everyone seems comfortable answering these two types of questions.

If Leon is 9, how old would someone 5 times as old be? (45)

How many years older than Leon is that person? (36 years)

Mei-Ling's grandmother is 6 times as old as Mei-Ling. How old is her grandmother? (66) How much older than Mei-Ling is she? (55 years)

Activity

Lifetime Strips

Demonstrating Lifetime Strips   Show the class the two strips of centimeter graph paper you prepared, representing the ages of an adult and of a child younger than the students you teach.

Here are two strips I made to represent the ages of two people in my life. This one *[hold up the shorter strip]* is 5 centimeters long to represent my daughter's age. She is 5 years old. This other strip represents my niece's age. She is 22 years old.

How could I use these strips to show how many times as old as my daughter my niece is? Here's another way we could ask that: How many of my daughter's lifetimes could fit into my niece's?

Hold the strips against each other as students direct. Count aloud together to keep track of how many times you move the shorter strip before it reaches the end of the longer strip. Take suggestions from students about how to describe the fractional part, in this case, 2 centimeters or two years. If no one suggests using fractions, bring up the idea yourself:

Some people would say "My niece is 4 and ⅖ times as old as my daughter."

Don't worry if some students don't seem to understand this now. They will have more chances to work with fractions when comparing their own family strips.

How can I use the strips to show *how many years older* my niece is than my daughter?

Again, act out what students suggest. If there is counting to be done, count aloud.

Making and Comparing Lifetime Strips Next, students will make their own lifetime strips for themselves and four adults. Then for the rest of Session 3, they will work with age comparisons on Student Sheet 23, Comparing Ages. Before sending students off to cut their strips, explain both parts of the activity so they can move straight into the age comparison work as they are ready.

Demonstrate how to use the one-centimeter graph paper, reminding students that 1 centimeter stands for 1 year.

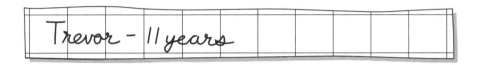

Make one strip to represent your own life. Then make strips for each of the four adults in your life whose ages you wrote down for homework. Label each strip with the name and age of the person whose lifetime it represents.

When they are finished, students should have five strips altogether.

After you have made all five strips, you're going to do the same kind of comparing ages with the people in your life as we did earlier with my daughter and my niece. You'll need to figure out the age difference two ways: (1) How many *times* as old as you is each of your adults? (2) How many years older than you are they? I'm going to hand out a sheet that has a chart to help you record your answers.

Distribute the one-centimeter graph paper and Student Sheet 23, Comparing Ages. Circulate as students make their five strips. Watch for students who are having trouble determining how long to make the strips. Encourage them to consult with others.

Most students' lifetime strips will not fit evenly into those of the adults. Expect and encourage students to struggle with how to deal with the "leftovers." If your class has done the *Investigations* grade 5 Fractions, Percents, and Decimals unit, *Name That Portion,* they will have some experience with these issues. If students draw conclusions such as "My mother is 3 times as old as me, and 4 centimeters more," ask:

What does the 4-centimeter length stand for? What part of one of your lifetimes is that?

Some students may try to estimate the leftover portion by "eyeballing it" and seeing, for example, that it is about a fourth, a half, or two-thirds of their own lifetime strip. Others may place their strip down one last time, then count the fraction of the strip that overlaps. For example, if the remainder is 7 cm and they are 11 years old, then the leftover fraction is 7/11. They can divide on a calculator to find the decimal. Some students may approximate the leftover portion, saying "a little over 3½ times." When many students are grappling with this same issue, come together and discuss some of the strategies students are using.

Dad - 40 years

Christine - 11 years
    Dad is 3 and $\frac{7}{11}$ times as old.
    Dad is a little over 3½ times as old.
    Dad is almost 4 times as old.

More Family Comparisons   Students who finish quickly can cut out a set of lifetime strips for their entire family and mount them on a piece of construction paper. If they know the ages of members of their extended family, they can include strips for them as well.

Students can also begin to make comparisons between different generations at the bottom of the student sheet or on the back. For example: How many times as old as your mother is your grandmother?

Activity

Choosing Student Work to Save

As the unit ends, you may want to use one of the following options for creating a record of students' work on this unit.

- Students look back through their folders or notebooks and write about what they learned in this unit, what they remember most, and what was hard or easy for them. You might have students do this work during their writing time.

- Students select one or two pieces of their work as their best work, and you also choose one or two pieces of their work, to be saved in a portfolio for the year. You might include students' written solutions to the assessments Describing the Measure of Weight and Liquid Quantity (p. 66) and A Year's Worth of Commercials (p. 82). Students can create a separate page with brief comments describing each piece of work.

■ You may want to send a selection of work home for families to see. Students write a cover letter, describing their work in this unit. This work should be returned if you are keeping year-long portfolios.

Session 3 Follow-Up

Comparing Ages Students take home their completed Student Sheet 23, Comparing Ages, to share what they have discovered with the adults whose ages they collected.

Making Historical Strips Pick the date of an invention or an historical event from your social studies or science curriculum. Students make time strips to represent the age of the invention or event. For example, if an invention is 112 years old, students create a strip that is one meter, twelve centimeters long. Students then find out how many times as old the invention is compared to themselves, and how many years older than they are it is.

Moving from Strips to Calculators Progressing from the visual to the abstract, students set aside their strips and use a calculator to compare lengths of time. For example, students might compare the age of their cat, grandmother, or school to the age of the United States (counting from the date the Declaration of Independence was signed, 1776). Some probable strategies to expect on the calculator include skip counting by the smaller age, approximating a number to multiply by the smaller age, and dividing the larger age by the smaller.

Representing a Millennium To represent 1000 years, post a ten-meter strip (1000 cm) of adding machine tape on a long stretch of wall, perhaps in the gym or hallway. Students can get a sense of how long ago that was by comparing their approximately 10-centimeter lifetime strips to the longer strip. To help them improve their sense of historical time, you might write important dates on this time line. Continue to help students see how these dates relate to their own experiences by asking questions like, "Do you know anyone who was alive when this took place?"

Estimation and Number Sense

Basic Activity

Students mentally estimate the answer to an arithmetic problem that they see displayed for about a minute. They discuss their estimates. Then they find a precise solution to the problem by using mental computation strategies.

Estimation and Number Sense provides opportunities for students to develop strategies for mental computation and for judging the reasonableness of the results of a computation done on paper or with a calculator. Students focus on:

- looking at a problem as a whole
- reordering or combining numbers within a problem for easier computation
- looking at the largest part of each number first (looking at hundreds before tens, thousands before hundreds, and so forth)

Materials

Calculators (for variation)

Procedure

Step 1. Present a problem on the chalkboard or overhead. For example:

$$9 + 25 + 11$$

Step 2. Allow 20 to 30 seconds for students to think about the problem. In this time, students come up with the best estimate they can for the solution. This solution might be, but does not have to be, an exact answer. Students do not write anything down or use the calculator during this time.

Step 3. Cover the problem and ask students to discuss what they know. Ask questions like these: "What did you notice about the numbers in this problem? Did you estimate an answer? How did you make your estimate?"

Encourage all kinds of estimation statements and strategies. Some will be more general; others may be quite precise: "It's at least 35 because I saw 25 and a number in the tens." "I think it's less than 100 because 25 was the biggest number and there were only three numbers." "I think it's 25 + 20 because I saw the 9 + 11 and that's 20 and then add on 25 and that gets you to 45."

Be sure that you continue to encourage a variety of observations, especially the "more than, less than" statements, even if some students have solved it exactly.

Step 4. Uncover the problem, allow another 30 seconds to solve it, and then continue the discussion. Ask further: "What do you notice now? What do you think about your estimates? Do you want to change them? What are some mental strategies you can use to solve the problem exactly?"

Variations

Problems That Can Be Reordered Give problems like the following, in which grouping the numbers in particular ways can help solve the problem easily:

$$6 + 2 - 4 + 1 - 5 + 4 + 5 - 2$$

$$36 + 22 + 4 + 8$$

$$112 - 30 + 60 - 2$$

$$654 - 12 + 300 + 112$$

Encourage students to look at the problem as a whole before they start to solve it. Rather than using each number and operation in sequence, they see what numbers are easy to put together to give answers to part of the problem. Then they combine their partial results to solve the whole problem.

Problems with Large Numbers Present problems that require students to "think from left to right" and to round numbers to "nice numbers" in order to come up with a good estimate. For example:

$130 + 243 + 492$	723
	481
$10,981 + 5,003 + 99,000$	$+\ 198$

Continued on next page

Present problems in both horizontal and vertical formats. If the vertical format triggers a rote procedure of starting from the right and "carrying," encourage students to look at the numbers as a whole, and to think about the largest parts of the numbers first. Thus, for the problem 130 + 243 + 492, they might think first, "492 is about 500." Then, thinking in terms of the largest part of the numbers first (hundreds), they might reason: "200 and 500 is 700, and 100 more is 800, and then there's some extra, so I think it's a little over 800."

Fractions   Pose problems using fractions and ask students to estimate the number of wholes the result is closest to. Start by posing problems such as $1/2 + 3/8$ or $1/2 + 3/4$, and ask, "Is the answer more than or less than 1?" Eventually, you can include fractions with larger results and expand the question to "Is the answer closer to 0, 1, or 2?" Begin to include problems such as $5 \times 1/4$ and $3 \times 1/8$. Use fractions such as $9/4$, $50/7$, $100/26$, or $63/20$, and ask, "About how many wholes are in this fraction?"

Decimals   Start by showing one decimal number at a time, such as 5.1248 or 23.87 or 14.47. Ask "about" what whole number it is, or if it is about halfway between two numbers. When students are familiar with interpreting individual decimal numbers, pose decimal problems. Ask them to estimate the number of wholes the result is closest to.

$5.17
$6.48
+ $3.30

$3.15 \times 521.123 \div 6.8$

$36.89 - 4.11$

Is It Bigger or Smaller?   Use any of the kinds of problems suggested above, but pose a question about the result to help students focus their estimation: "Is this bigger than 20? Is it smaller than $10.00? If I have $20.00, do I have enough to buy these four things?"

Using the Calculator   The calculator can be used to check results. Emphasize that it is easy to make mistakes on a calculator. Sometimes you press the wrong number or the wrong operation. Sometimes you leave out a number, or a key

sticks and doesn't register. However, people who are good at using the calculator always make a mental estimate so they can tell whether their result is reasonable. Pose some problems like this one:

I was adding 212, 357, and 436 on my calculator. The answer I got was 615. Was that a reasonable answer? Why or why not?

Include problems in which the result is reasonable and problems in which it is not. When the answer is unreasonable, some students might be interested in figuring out what happened. For example, in the above case, the user accidentally entered 46 instead of 436.

Parts of Wholes   Students use calculators to find many multiplication problems that have a certain answer. Pick a target number that has many factors (such as 12, 18, 20, 24, 30, 36, 60). Ask, "What multiplication problems can you do to get 20 as an answer?" Students will probably give some whole-number problems, such as 4×5 or 2×10. Write down their solutions and ask if they can think of any that use fractions ($1/3$ of what number is 20?). Using the calculator with fractions sometimes leads to approximate numbers: $1 \div 3 \times 60$ or 0.3333333×60 will result in a display of 19.999998, but students should recognize this as close to the exact answer, in this case 20.

Problems with Many Numbers   Students invent a problem with many numbers that must be added and subtracted. Students show how they can reorder the numbers in the problem to make it easier to solve. They solve the problem using two different methods to double-check their solution. One way might be using the calculator. Here is an example of such a problem:

$30 - 6 + 92 - 20 + 56 + 70 + 8$

Save students' problems to use in Ten-Minute Math sessions.

Guess My Number

Note: The Ten-Minute Math activities suggested for this unit involve Guess My Unit, a variation of the Guess My Number activity (p. 96).

Basic Activity

You choose a number for students to guess, and start by giving clues about the characteristics of the number. For example: It is less than 50. It is a multiple of 7. One of its digits is 2 more than the other digit.

Students work in pairs to try to identify the number. Record students' suggested solutions on the board and invite them to challenge any solutions they don't agree with. If more than one solution fits the clues, encourage students to ask more questions to narrow the field. They might ask, for example: Is the number less than 40? Is the number a multiple of 5?

Guess My Number involves students in logical reasoning as they apply the clues to choose numbers that fit and to eliminate those that don't. Students also investigate aspects of number theory as they learn to recognize and describe the characteristics of numbers and relationships among numbers. Students' work focuses on:

- systematically eliminating possibilities
- using evidence
- formulating questions to logically eliminate possible solutions
- recognizing relationships among numbers, such as which are multiples or factors of each other
- learning to use mathematical terms that describe numbers
- sorting measuring units

Materials

- 100 chart or 300 chart (optional)
- Scraps of paper or numeral cards for showing solutions (optional)
- Calculators (for variation)
- Guess My Unit cards (pp. 125–126), cut into decks (one per group, for Guess My Unit)

Procedure

Step 1. Choose a number. You may want to write it down so that you don't forget what you picked.

Step 2. Give students clues. Sometimes, you might choose clues so that only one solution is possible. Other times, you might choose clues so that several solutions are possible. Use clues that describe number characteristics and relationships, such as factors, multiples, the number of digits, and odd and even.

Step 3. Students work in pairs to find numbers that fit the clues. A 100 chart (or 300 chart for larger numbers) and scraps of paper or numeral cards are useful for recording numbers they think might fit. Give students just one or two minutes to find numbers they think might work.

Step 4. Record all suggested solutions. To get responses from every student, you may want to ask students to record their solutions on scraps of paper and hold them up on a given signal. Some teachers provide numeral cards that students can hold up to show their solution (for example, they might hold up a 2 and a 1 together to show 21). List on the board all solutions that students propose. Students look over all the proposed solutions and challenge any they think don't fit all the clues. They should give the reasons for their challenges.

Step 5. Invite students to ask further questions. If more than one solution fits all the clues, let students ask yes-or-no questions to try to eliminate some of the possibilities, until only one solution remains. You can erase numbers as students' questions eliminate them (be sure to ask students to tell you which numbers you should erase). Encourage students to ask questions that might eliminate more than one of the proposed solutions.

Continued on next page

Variations

New Number Characteristics During the year, vary this game to include mathematical terms that describe numbers or relationships among numbers that have come up in mathematics class. For example, include factors, multiples, doubling (tripling, halving), square numbers, prime numbers, odd and even numbers, less than and more than concepts, as well as the number of digits in a number.

Large Numbers Begin with numbers under 100, but gradually expand the range of numbers that you include in your clues to larger numbers with which your students have been working. For example:

> It is a multiple of 50. It has 3 digits. Two of its digits are the same. It is not a multiple of 100.

Guess My Fraction Pick a fraction. Tell students whether it is smaller than 1/2, between 1/2 and 1, between 1 and 2, or bound by any other familiar numbers. You might use clues like these:

> It is a multiple of 1/4 (for example, 1/2, 3/4, 1 whole, 1 1/4).

> The numerator is 2 (for example, 2/3, 2/5).

> You can make it with pattern blocks (for example, 2/3, 5/6).

Guess My Unit In this version of the game, students use logical reasoning to guess a particular unit of measurement. Select a measurement unit on the cards or choose one of your own. If you create a new card, be sure to add that card to each set. Each pair or group of students should have a complete set of Guess My Unit cards, displayed faceup on their desks.

Follow the procedure for the basic game. Give students a few beginning clues that focus on the characteristics and relationships among measurement units. For example: It is a measurement of weight. It is a metric unit. It is more than twice as much as a pound.

Record the initial clues where students can refer to them. Give students a few minutes to work together to try to discover your unit. They may flip over or set aside any cards that your clues have eliminated as possibilities. They may then ask yes-or-no questions until they can identify the unit.

Calculator Guess My Number Present clues that provide opportunities for computation using a calculator. For example:

> It is larger than 35×20. It is smaller than $1800 \div 2$. One of its factors is 25. None of its digits is 7.

Don't Share Solutions Until the End As students become more practiced in formulating questions to eliminate possible solutions, you may want to skip step 4. That is, student pairs find all solutions they think are possible, but these are not shared and posted. Rather, in a whole-class discussion, students ask yes-or-no questions, but privately eliminate numbers (or measurement units) on their own list of solutions. When students have no more questions, they volunteer their solutions and explain why they think their answer is correct.

Students' Secret Numbers Each student chooses a number or unit and develops clues to present to the rest of the class. You'll probably want to have students submit their numbers and clues for your review in advance. If the clues are too broad (for example, 50 solutions are possible) or don't work, ask the students to revise their clues. Once you approve the clues, students are in charge of presenting them, running the discussion, and answering all questions about their number during a Ten-Minute Math session.

The following activities will help ensure that this unit is comprehensible to students who are acquiring English as a second language. The suggested approach is based on *The Natural Approach: Language Acquisition in the Classroom* by Stephen D. Krashen and Tracy D. Terrell (Alemany Press, 1983). The intent is for second-language learners to acquire new vocabulary in an active, meaningful context.

Note that *acquiring* a word is different from *learning* a word. Depending on their level of proficiency, students may be able to comprehend a word upon hearing it during an investigation, without being able to say it. Other students may be able to use the word orally, but not read or write it. The goal is to help students naturally acquire targeted vocabulary at their present level of proficiency.

We suggest using these activities just before the related investigations. The activities can also be led by English-proficient students.

Investigation 1

scale, pound, weight, weighs, estimate, exact, precise

1. Identify a *scale* (use a bathroom scale) as you place it in front of students. Choose a student to stand next to it.

2. Tell the group that you will *estimate* this student's *weight*. Exaggerate eyeing the student from head to toe. After a few seconds, nod and say your estimate.

   I estimate Duc weighs 62 pounds.

   Write your estimate on the board.

3. Now ask the student to stand on the scale. Have students note the *exact* or *precise* weight. Ask them to compare this number to your estimate.

4. Continue the activity, but challenge the group to do the initial estimating.

5. Introduce and demonstrate the use of a balance scale for weighing smaller objects.

personal

1. Show students your comb, combing your hair with it. Explain:

This is my comb. It is my personal comb. No one else may use it. *[With gestures, exaggerate keeping your comb away from the students.]*

2. Pick up a classroom pencil and write something with it. Then hand it to a student as you explain:

   This is *not* my personal pencil. Anyone may use it.

3. Continue to identify articles of jewelry or apparel and other classroom objects as being either your *personal* belonging or not. Ask the students to identify something of theirs that is personal.

Investigation 2

product, bottle, can, box, containers

1. Have available several grocery products packaged in different containers (for example, cans of fruit and soup, bottles of cooking oil and soda, boxes of crackers and cake mix. Identify each product and how it is packaged.

   This product is pineapple chunks. *[Outline the can with your finger.]* **It is packaged in a can.**

2. Model how to group the products by type of container.

   These products *[point]* **are packaged in different containers. Some are in bottles** *[point]*, **some in boxes** *[point]*, **and some in cans** *[point]*. **Let's group these products by type of container.**

3. Challenge the students to respond with the names of the containers as you ask simple questions.

   Which of these is the largest container? Which container might break if you drop it? Which containers are round? *[Use your finger to indicate roundness.]* **Which containers have square corners?** *[Draw a square in the air with your finger.]*

space (amount of space something takes up)

1. Show students a shallow empty container, such as a basket. Put your hand inside and indicate how much room there is.

   There is lots of space in this basket. We can put things inside to fill the space.

Continued on next page

2. Put an object in the basket.

Does this fill all the space? Is there more space inside?

3. Continue packing objects into the basket until it is full. Explain:

These things take up all the space in the basket.

4. Ask students to remove items from the basket in response to questions about how much space they take up.

Which thing takes up the most space? Which takes up the least space?

liquid

1. As you display a glass filled with water, a glass ¾ full of juice, and a glass ¼ full of milk, identify each liquid.

The liquid in this glass is water. The liquid in this glass is juice. The liquid in this last glass is milk.

2. Ask questions about the amount of liquid in each glass.

Which liquid almost fills the glass? Which liquid fills less than half the glass? Which liquids fill more than half the glass?

Blackline Masters

_____ , 19 ____

Dear Family,

We are beginning a mathematics unit called *Measurement Benchmarks.* In this unit, your child will learn how to estimate and measure length, distance, weight, liquid quantities, and time. Along the way, your child will learn how *benchmarks* can help us get a good sense of measurement.

You might have your own benchmarks. What do you imagine when you think of a centimeter? a pound? a kilogram? a quart? For instance, you might know that your index fingernail is a centimeter wide, or that your small saucepan holds about a quart. Whatever benchmarks work for you, your child will find his or her own.

Throughout this unit, your child will be working with two measurement systems: the U.S. standard system (including measures such as quarts, miles, and pounds), and the metric system (including measures such as liters, kilometers, and kilograms).

Your child will sometimes be asked to gather information at home. You can help in several ways:

- Show how you use measurement—with rulers, measuring cups, or other specialized tools.

- Talk to your child about the metric system. Do you think the United States should convert entirely to the metric system? Why or why not?

- When the homework asks for grocery products that show measurement on their labels, help your child look at home or in the market for the measures of weight and volume on cans, packages, containers, and bottles. Also look on product labels to identify where the product comes from. Is it from someplace near, or very far away? Are most of the foods you eat grown or produced nearby? Are any of them grown or produced at least 500 miles away? at least 1000 miles away?

We hope you will enjoy working with your child to become more familiar with measurement and the many ways we use it.

Sincerely,

Exploring Measurement

Length

Use a ruler. Find something that is about a foot long. Describe it:

Use a ruler. Find something that is about a centimeter long.
Describe it:

Use a meterstick. Find something that is about a meter long.
Describe it:

Time

Use a clock or watch. Find something that takes about a minute to do. Describe it:

Weight

Use a balance scale and a kilogram weight. Find something that weighs about a kilogram. Describe it:

Use a balance scale and a pound weight. Find something that weighs about a pound.
Describe it:

Liquid Quantity

Use sand or water and a liter measure. Find a container that holds about a liter.
Describe the container:

Use sand or water and a cup measure. Find a container that holds about a cup.
Describe the container:

Benchmark Estimates

Object	Benchmark estimates	Why estimates differ	Measurement

When and How Do You Measure?

Interview one or more adults at home to find at least three situations in which they measure. Look for times when they measure with tools (for example, using a tape measure) and times when they estimate (for example, adding a pinch of salt). Write each situation in one of the boxes below.

These questions may help you with the interview:

- What are some times when you use measurement?
- What things do you try to measure exactly?
- What tools do you use?
- When do you use only *about* the right measure, or an estimate?
- How do you do it?

Situation 1	Situation 2
Situation 3	Situation 4

(If you interview more than one person, record the information in boxes on a fresh piece of paper or on note cards. Do not write the information on the back of this student sheet.)

How Tall Is an Adult?

Ask an adult outside of class for his or her height,
and then write it in the space below. You can record the
adult's height either in feet and inches or in centimeters. You
will need this information in class tomorrow.

Name of person: _____

Height of person: _____

Explaining Measurement Differences

1. Record all the measurements your class found for the length of the classroom.

2. What is one of the smallest measurements? _____

3. Why do you think some people got smaller measurements?

4. What is one of the largest measurements? _____

5. Why do you think some people got larger measurements?

Sharing Measurement Data

Take the paper strip you cut and measured in class to the adult whose height you recorded. Explain what you know about the person's height in both feet and inches, and in centimeters.

In the chart below, list any benchmarks you use for the following units. A *benchmark* is something familiar that is about the same size as a given unit of measurement (for example, a centimeter is about the width of a regular paper clip).

Unit	Abbreviation	Benchmark You Use
inch	in or "	
foot	ft or '	
yard	yd	
centimeter	cm	
meter	m	

Should the U.S. Go Metric?

Interview an adult outside of school. Ask the following questions:

Do you think it makes sense for the United States to convert to metric? Why or why not?

Record the adult's responses on the back of this page. You might write them in the form of a brief newspaper article with a list of pros and cons.

Preparation

We are going to be studying measures of weight and liquid volume soon. Please bring two grocery items to school.

Try to bring one package, can, or bottle with the *weight* (pounds, ounces, grams) of the contents on its label, and one with the *liquid volume* (liters, milliliters, quarts, pints, fluid ounces) of the contents on its label.

The item with weight on its label must be full. The item with liquid volume on its label can be full or empty.

We will use these items in school for a few days. Put your name on anything that you want to bring back home.

How Far Products Travel

Product	Where it comes from	About how far away

How Far Away?

On the shelves at home or at a market, look for the product that you think traveled the least distance and the one that you think traveled the farthest to reach you. Record the information below. You can figure out the actual distance your product traveled on the map at school.

Least Distance

I think _____
                              name of product
traveled the least distance to reach me.

It traveled from _____ .
                              name of the place where the product comes from

(Fill this part out in school.)

It only had to travel _____ to reach me.
                              the actual distance your product traveled

Farthest Distance

I think _____
                              name of product
traveled the farthest distance to reach me.

It traveled from _____ .
                              name of the place where the product comes from

(Fill this part out in school.)

It had to travel _____ to reach me.
                              the actual distance your product traveled

How Much Does It Weigh?

	Weight of Contents	
Product	Metric measure 1 kilogram (kg) = 1000 grams (g)	U.S. standard measure 1 pound (lb) = 16 ounces (oz)

How do metric measures and U.S. standard measures compare?
Write about something you found out. For example, how many
grams are in a pound? Which is larger, a pound or a kilogram?

HOMEWORK
Find one product that looks small but has a large weight.
Find another product that looks large but has a small weight.

Record the information in the last two rows of the table.

How Much Liquid Inside?

Quantity of Liquid Contents		
Product	Metric measure 1 liter (l) = 1000 milliliter (ml) 1 milliliter = 1 cubic centimeter (cc)	U.S. standard measure 1 cup = 8 fl oz 1 pint (pt) = 16 fl oz 1 quart (qt) = 32 fl oz 4 quarts = 1 gallon (gal)

How do metric measures and U.S. standard measures compare? Write about something you found out. For example, which is larger, a liter or a quart? About how many milliliters are in a pint?

HOMEWORK
On your shelves at home, find the product with the largest liquid quantity. Then find the one with the smallest liquid quantity. Record what you find in the last two rows of the table.

Vegetable Weights

1. Visit the market. Go to the produce section and find
    the scales there.

2. Choose at least 5 of the following fruits and vegetables.
    If you can do more, great! (Some may not be available.)

3. Find a typical-looking vegetable.

4. Put the vegetable on the scale. Record how much
    it weighs. Weigh it to the nearest quarter pound.
    For example, if it weighs between 1 and 2 pounds,
    write one of these:

    1 lb $1\frac{1}{4}$ lb $1\frac{1}{2}$ lb $1\frac{3}{4}$ lb   2 lb

    On a metric scale, weigh to the nearest 100 g.

5. Write the weight next to the name of each vegetable
    you weighed.

 cabbage _____   pumpkin _____

 cauliflower _____   tomato _____

 lettuce _____   watermelon _____

 potato _____   zucchini _____

Comparing Weights

Part 1
Find something that balances each of the weights below.
Describe what you find for each weight.

1 kilogram _____

500 grams _____

100 grams _____

1 gram _____

1 pound _____

1 ounce _____

Part 2
Use your weights to find out which is heavier. Then write
how you could prove it using labels on packages.

1. Which is heavier, a kilogram or a pound?

2. Which is heavier, 500 grams or a pound?

3. Which is heavier, an ounce or a gram?

4. Write the six weights in order, starting with the lightest.

Things I Know About a Kilogram

Think about what you already know about a kilogram.
Record at least 5 things you know in the spaces below.
Use words, number sentences, and/or sketches. Include
a description of your benchmarks(s) for a kilogram.

1.

2.

3.

4.

5.

Comparing Liquid Quantities

Part 1
Find something that holds each of the quantities below.
Describe the container for each quantity.

1 liter _____

500 milliliters _____

1 quart _____

1 cup _____

1 fluid ounce _____

Part 2
Use your liquid measures to find out which is more. Then
write how you could prove it using labels on packages.

1. Which is more, a quart or a liter?

2. Which is more, 500 milliliters or 1 cup?

3. How many milliliters are in one-fourth of a liter?

4. How many milliliters are in a liter?

5. Write the five liquid quantities in order, starting
   with the smallest.

Things I Know About a Liter

Think about what you already know about a liter. In the spaces below, record at least 5 things you know. Use words, number sentences, and/or sketches. Include a description of your benchmark(s) for a liter.

1.

2.

3.

4.

5.

Feathers or Bricks?

Ask someone outside of school the following riddle:

> **Which weighs more, a pound of feathers or
> a pound of bricks?**

Write down the person's answer and his or her reasoning.

_____

_____

_____

_____

Make up a variation on this riddle (or more if you want)
using other materials.

Record-Breaker Vegetables

Vegetable	Our typical weight	Record-breaker	Number of times as heavy as our typical weight
Cabbage		124 pounds (56 kilograms)	
Cauliflower		53 pounds (24 kilograms)	
Lettuce		25 pounds (11 kilograms)	
Potato		7 pounds (3 kilograms)	
Pumpkin		817 pounds (371 kilograms)	
Tomato		8 pounds (4 kilograms)	
Watermelon		262 pounds (119 kilograms)	
Zucchini		65 pounds (29 kilograms)	

Record-breaker vegetable data from National Geographic *WORLD*, copyright October 1991 National Geographic Society. Data rounded to nearest pound or kilogram.

Making Record-Breaker Benchmarks

Make your own benchmarks for at least three record-breaker vegetables.

1. The record-breaker_____ weighs _____

   That is about as heavy as_____

2. The record-breaker_____ weighs _____

   That is about as heavy as_____

3. The record-breaker_____ weighs _____

   That is about as heavy as_____

4. The record-breaker_____ weighs _____

   That is about as heavy as_____

Estimating 30 Seconds

1. In the space below, make a graph of your estimates. Your graph should show your estimates in the order you made them.

2. Describe in words how your estimates changed with practice.

3. What advice would you give to help someone else estimate 30 seconds?

Commercial Minutes

Gather data on the number of commercial minutes
in any half-hour television show. Use a clock or watch
that shows seconds. Begin timing exactly on the hour
or half hour.

Name of show _____

Day of week _____

Time it began _____

Time the show stopped for commercials	Time the show started again	Number of commercial minutes

Total number of commercial minutes _____

Adults' Ages

Find out the ages of four adults outside of school. Try
to find both older and younger adults. Write down the
name and age of each person in the space below.

	Name of Person	Age of Person
1.		
2.		
3.		
4.		

Comparing Ages

I was born in ——————————. I am ———— years old.
                    (year)

Who?	How old?	How many years older than you?	How many times as old as you?

Duplicate a set of cards, on card stock if possible, for each pair or small group.
Use the blank cards to add other units of measurement that may have come up in class.

If you have students with limited English proficiency, help them identify each unit and
draw a simple picture on the card—such as a benchmark they found in class—that
will help them identify that unit as they are playing the Guess My Unit game.

mile	**foot**	**inch**
meter	**centimeter**	**millimeter**
kilometer		

pound	**ounce**	**ton**
kilogram	**gram**	**milligram**

quart	cup	fluid ounce
liter	milliliter	cubic centimeter

second	minute	hour
day	week	month
year	decade	century

Practice Pages

This optional section provides homework ideas for teachers who want or need to give more homework than is assigned to accompany the activities in this unit. The problems included here provide additional practice in learning about number relationships and in solving computation and number problems. For number units, you may want to use some of these if your students need more work in these areas or if you want to assign daily homework. For other units, you can use these problems so that students can continue to work on developing number and computation sense while they are focusing on other mathematical content in class. We recommend that you introduce activities in class before assigning related problems for homework.

Digits Game   This game is introduced in the unit *Building on Numbers You Know.* If your students are familiar with the game, you can simply send home the directions, score sheet, and Numeral Cards so that students can play at home. If your students have not played this game before, introduce it in class and have students play once or twice before sending it home. In the beginning, ask students to work with 4-digit targets such as 1000, 2500, or 6723. Later, they can try 5-digit targets such as 10,000, 59,500, and 30,000. You might have students do this activity two or three times for homework in this unit.

Counting Up   In this activity, introduced in the unit *Building on Numbers You Know,* students write the numbers they would say if they counted up by a given number. Provided here are two work sheets. Because this activity is included in the curriculum only as homework, it is recommended that you briefly introduce it in class before students work on it at home.

Story Problems   Story problems at various levels of difficulty are used throughout the *Investigations* curriculum. The two story problem sheets provided here help students review and maintain skills that have already been taught. You can make up other problems in this format, using numbers and contexts that are appropriate for your students. Students solve the problems and then record their strategies.

How to Play the Digits Game

Materials: Numeral Cards (with Wild Cards removed)
Digits Game Score Sheet

Players: 2 or 3

How to Play

1. Decide on the target number to use.

   Example: The target is 1000.

2. Deal the Numeral Cards. Deal out one more card than there are digits in the target.

   Example: The target has four digits, so you deal out five cards: 3, 8, 0, 1, and 5.

3. Players use the numerals on the cards to make a number as close as possible to the target.

   Example: You can use 3, 8, 0, 1, and 5 to make 1035, 853, or other numbers.

4. Write the target and the number you made on your score sheet. Find and record the difference between them.

   Example: $1000 - 853 = 147$. The difference is your score.

5. When everyone has finished, compare answers. Which number is closest to the target? Is it possible to make a number even closer?

   Example: Player A made 853. Player B made 1305. Who is closer? Can you make a number with these digits that is even closer to 1000?

6. For the next round, mix up all the cards and deal a new set.

7. After three rounds, total your scores. Lowest total wins.

Digits Game Score Sheet

For each round you play, record the target number and the closest number you can make with your digits. Put the larger one first. Then find and record the difference between them.

PLAYER A

Game target: _____   Difference

Round 1: _____ – _____ = _____

Round 2: _____ – _____ = _____

Round 3: _____ – _____ = _____

Total score: _____

PLAYER B

Game target: _____   Difference

Round 1: _____ – _____ = _____

Round 2: _____ – _____ = _____

Round 3: _____ – _____ = _____

Total score: _____

PLAYER C

Game target: _____   Difference

Round 1: _____ – _____ = _____

Round 2: _____ – _____ = _____

Round 3: _____ – _____ = _____

Total score: _____

0	0	1	1
0	0	1	1
2	2	3	3
2	2	3	3

130

4	4	5	5
4	4	5	5
<u>6</u>	<u>6</u>	7	7
<u>6</u>	<u>6</u>	7	7

8	8	<u>9</u>	<u>9</u>
8	8	<u>9</u>	<u>9</u>
WILD CARD	**WILD CARD**		
WILD CARD	**WILD CARD**		

Practice Page A

Fill in the numbers you say if you start at 100 and
count up by each counting number.

Count up by 5	Count up by 10	Count up by 50	Count up by 250	Count up by _____ (your choice)
100	100	100	100	100
_____	_____	_____	_____	_____
_____	_____	_____	_____	_____
_____	_____	_____	_____	_____
_____	_____	_____	_____	_____
_____	_____	_____	_____	_____
_____	_____	_____	_____	_____
_____	_____	_____	_____	_____
_____	_____	_____	_____	_____
_____	_____	_____	_____	_____
_____	_____	_____	_____	_____
_____	_____	_____	_____	_____
_____	_____	_____	_____	_____

Practice Page
Measurement Benchmarks

Practice Page B

Fill in the numbers you say if you start at 200 and count
up by each counting number.

Count up by 5	Count up by 10	Count up by 50	Count up by 250	Count up by _____ (your choice)
200	200	200	200	200
_____	_____	_____	_____	_____
_____	_____	_____	_____	_____
_____	_____	_____	_____	_____
_____	_____	_____	_____	_____
_____	_____	_____	_____	_____
_____	_____	_____	_____	_____
_____	_____	_____	_____	_____
_____	_____	_____	_____	_____
_____	_____	_____	_____	_____
_____	_____	_____	_____	_____
_____	_____	_____	_____	_____

Practice Page C

For each problem, show how you found your solution.

Suppose there is a new coin called the quarto.
A quarto is worth 24 cents.

1. How many quartos are in 1 dollar?

2. How many quartos are in 2 dollars?

3. How many quartos are in 5 dollars?

Practice Page D

For each problem, show how you found your solution.

Suppose that pencils come in boxes of six.

1. If there are 15 boxes in the supply room, how many pencils are there in all?

2. If there are 22 boxes in the supply room, how many pencils are there in all?

3. If there are 30 boxes in the supply room, how many pencils are there in all?